TAKE HEART

TAKE HEART

HOPEFUL & HUMOROUS LESSONS
FROM A TWO-TIME TRANSPLANT RECIPIENT

David Craig

 **Ripples Media**

"David Craig's *Take Heart* is a remarkable testament to resilience and the human spirit. David's journey, marked by his unwavering faith and profound gratitude for the gift of life, offers invaluable lessons on navigating adversity with grace and humor. His ability to transform challenging moments into opportunities for growth and connection is truly inspiring. This book is a heartfelt guide for anyone seeking hope and strength in the face of life's toughest trials."

Ken Bernhardt
Regents Professor Emeritus, Georgia State University

"David's journey transcends mere survival. His unwavering optimism, discipline, and perseverance have given us a roadmap for embracing hope and living purposefully—even when the challenges seem insurmountable. I witnessed his strength both at work and in church, and his story continues to inspire me every day."

Rilla Delorier
Former Chief Marketing Officer at SunTrust Bank, Board Director for: Atlantic Union Bank, Coastal Community Bank, WisdomTree Investments, and Nymbus

Published by Ripples Media
www.ripples.media

First printing 2025

Book and cover designed by Burtch Hunter

979-8-9986533-1-5 Paperback
979-8-9986533-2-2 Hardback
979-8-9986533-0-8 E-book

Dedicated to my wife Sandy,
who has been on this rollercoaster of life
for the past twenty-five-plus years,
and to our kids Owen and Julia.

Contents

Foreword

by Bob Carter

Area Pastor, Perimeter Church, Duluth, Georgia

I often think of people who have resiliency or as some people have referred to it, as grit. These folks tend to be tough-minded through tough times. I wonder are they just born that way or do they learn to be resilient? I don't know. All I can say is David Craig has it. He has resiliency; he has grit.

I first met David at church. He and I were a part of a men's small group which met to talk about the Bible and encourage one another in the faith. On occasion, David would calmly discuss a physical challenge or diagnosis, as if he was saying he had a common cold. I'd listen, asking myself, "How is this guy not incredibly depressed?" Was he depressed? Oh, I'm sure he had his moments, but after a while, I thought, "You can't fake this." He would easily talk about another life hurdle, look at the next step, and move forward.

He accepted what was before him. I guess in some ways that's what resiliency looks like.

Being around David, I've observed a pretty humble guy. He doesn't like to draw attention to himself and even with this book, it's ultimately not about him. I guess what he has shown me is a bigger story going on.

Years ago, author Madelyn L'Engle wrote, "I have a point of view. You have a point of view. God has view." She was saying we are finite, but God is infinite. There is a bigger story going on, which is God's purpose in our life. We often just see our circumstances (good or bad), but for God, the circumstances are a part of something much bigger: His purpose is that we reflect His character. To have view is to begin seeing things from God's perspective. Sometimes, I think God has given David Craig a bit more view, to see this life from a bigger or broader aspect. David calls it an eternal perspective.

The Bible says we see in a mirror dimly. Yes, in this life, we often don't have view, and our vision is somewhat obstructed. We get glimpses of eternity but God gives us people who help us see a bit more clearly, so we have view. David is one of these. I hope in reading his story, perhaps you gain a bit more resiliency, more grit, and more view.

The Resilient Heart

by Susan Somersille Johnson

Former Global CMO, Prudential Financial
Former CMO, SunTrust Banks, Inc.

David's remarkable journey is one that only a few have ever experienced—fewer still have lived to tell. His story is one of unimaginable pain, extraordinary courage, and unshakable hope. Yet through it all, David does more than persevere and survive, David thrives.

As a top executive for a large financial services company, David has achieved more than most can dream of, despite, or perhaps because of, his health challenges. He is a rock for his family, his church, his community, and his colleagues . . . like me. He is an inspiring example of living fully in the face of adversity.

When I met David, I had just joined the executive leadership team of a major financial services organization in Atlanta. After several roles outside of the country, I was ready to dig in and focus on helping improve the lives of our clients in the US. The task of leading a large marketing, digital, and communications organization was daunting, and choosing the team was vital. For an organization in the growth phase, every role was key.

Upon meeting David, I was immediately struck by his bright disposition, which seems to defy the countless surgeries that have reshaped his handsome face. He is fit, standing firm and at attention like a soldier in training—no wincing, no sighing, no outward signs of the pain that has almost certainly been a constant companion. His strength is not just physical, but also emotional and spiritual.

David is a results-oriented leader and had already built a strong reputation in business marketing. So I decided to ask him to continue to lead the group while I shored up other functions. Over the next six years that we worked together, David's contribution to our team far exceeded his outstanding results. He has had a deeper and more profound impact on all of our lives.

We learned quickly that David has the uncanny ability to transcend and transform the moments he is in . . . because every single moment matters to him. He embodies "don't sweat the small stuff" because, from marketing crisis to crisis, he was the steady voice of reason. Through it all, his unwavering faith has served as both an anchor and stabilizing force.

One of our teammates reminded me of a story that exemplifies how David makes it possible for us to laugh at anything. She was talking to David as he was preparing for a particularly tough meeting. It was a difficult time in our industry, so frustration was mounting. The tone was tense and people were anxiously dealing with uncertainty. David was asked to meet with a leader who had just taken a new role. This leader had a reputation as extremely abrasive, opinionated, and harsh—not someone you look forward to presenting to. Yet, David, who is extremely competitive, rose to the challenge and was in good spirits as he prepared his message and slides.

After the meeting, she bumped into David coming out of the elevator and asked him, "How'd it go?" David said, "It went OK." "Tell me more." David told her that as he walked the leader through the slides, as anticipated, he was his usual combative self—his eyes glazed over, he cut David off dismissively, and he said, "we're done here." He ended the meeting early and said, "Don't ever bring me slides again." Our colleague asked David, "It doesn't sound like it went OK?" Then, with enthusiasm and optimism, David told her, "I've got him right where I want him."

This is how, over time, David became known as the Ultimate Comeback Kid. He is so well grounded in what he can change, what he can't, and what's worth worrying about. We were always laughing at his one-liners. For example, after his face surgeries, "I have a face for radio" and "Thank God I'm already married."

David speaks often of the responsibility he feels in caring for such a precious gift. He views it as divine, often quoting the verse from Ezekiel 36:26, shared with him by his pastor before his first surgery many years ago:

"And I will give you a new heart and a new spirit I will put within you. And I will remove the heart of stone from your flesh and give you a heart of flesh."

David carries the weight of this verse with him daily, mindful of the two twenty-year-old donors whose hearts have allowed him to live. He is deeply grateful and feels a profound responsibility to be a worthy recipient and steward of this miraculous gift.

I also extend my deepest condolences to the families of those donors. While I can never truly understand the depth of their loss, I hope they find comfort in knowing that David has honored their gift in the most meaningful way possible. I could not imagine a more worthy person to receive such a gift.

This is why when we learned that David was about to mark the 30th anniversary of his heart, and that it was the third oldest transplanted heart in the country, we knew we had to celebrate in a big way. He had been through countless challenges since he became one of the youngest people to have a successful heart transplant, challenges that for most of us, would have knocked us on our back, tanked our careers and our relationships. Yet David had built a strong family and risen to become a respected leader in a large, competitive organization.

We decided to plan a surprise party. The night before, one of our colleagues made "I Heart David" t-shirts by hand at home in her craft room. We asked his wife Sandy to see how she could keep the secret, yet show up with the kids. We invited the entire marketing team, colleagues from finance, risk, HR and other teams, and partners who lived around the US and other countries.

Everyone came. We wanted to celebrate David and thank him for the many lessons he shared, for his strength, grace, and inspiring example of what it means to live fully in the face of adversity. And I don't know how she managed it, but Sandy and the kids showed up, and he was completely surprised. Oh how we partied that day!

One story that perfectly exemplifies David's character comes from another teammate. His mother had passed away and our colleague told us he would be taking time off to manage the arrangements. "I'm going to be a C player for a while, until I get through this." He invited the team to the funeral service, but David unfortunately had a conflict and could not attend.

As our teammate was driving around his hometown, planning for the services, someone from the funeral home called and told him a co-worker was sitting quietly in a corner of the viewing room. David had driven four hours from Atlanta to Columbia, South Carolina, to show his respect and offer support—no fanfare, no fuss—just a quiet, meaningful presence. He called David and said, "Don't go anywhere, I'm coming to you." David asked him not to bother as he understood he had family and friends to be with, and David only had a few minutes before he had to turn around and drive back four hours.

He convinced David to wait, and when they embraced, David only shared one thought: "Your mother would be proud." That is David in a nutshell—a constant source of class and grace, always going out of his way to affirm the importance of human connections and the moments that truly matter.

I often sit in awe of the medical science that made the first successful human heart transplant possible in 1967. It is this same science that has allowed us to continue to have David in our lives. I can scarcely imagine the journey, the challenges, and the miracles of those who have lived through such an experience, but I am blessed to have worked alongside David, who continues to touch and inspire all who have the privilege of knowing him.

This book is a gift—crafted from the intersection of science, hope, and pain. It serves as a powerful reminder that life's challenges are not defined by what happens to us, but by how we respond to them.

My hope for you, the reader, is that David inspires you as much as he inspires me. Throughout my career, having led marketing teams supporting 180 countries, I have met a lot of people—across cultures and continents. The most meaningful thing I have learned is that we are more alike than we are different. So I know that whatever you're going through, whatever challenges you face, you will find strength and guidance in these pages—not just to survive, but to live life to the fullest!

Introduction

I recently read an article by *Wall Street Journal* opinion columnist Peggy Noonan titled "The Uglification of Everything." She writes about the current ugliness that pervades our culture. She references how remakes of two classic movies—"The Talented Mr. Ripley" and "Cabaret"—took clever films with brilliant acting and turned them into "grimy, gloomy, grim" experiences. Her final thought:

"Because even though it isn't new, uglification is rising and spreading as an artistic attitude, and it can't be good for us. Because it speaks of self-hatred, and a society that hates itself won't last. Because it gives those who are young nothing to love and feel soft about. Because we need beauty to keep our morale up."

How do we change that? How can we swim upstream to optimism when downstream is uglification and pessimism? For twenty years, people have told me I should write a book about how I maintain hope, optimism, and humor when my downstream is significant health challenges. As I recover from my second heart transplant—thirty-five years after the first—I have decided that it is high time to write about the hope that sustains me.

People around me see how I live through extremely difficult health experiences yet continue to maintain a positive outlook on life. This is not by chance. It's because of discipline and a belief that God has a perfect plan for my life, including all of my positive, neutral, and negative experiences. Some of my most challenging health experiences have been:

1988	First heart transplant.
1990	Colitis. Foot of colon removed.
1991	Gall stones. Gall bladder removed.
1997-2024	More than 100 Mohs skin cancer surgeries.
2005-2010	Five skin cancer tumor surgeries that paralyzed the left side of my face.
2012	Emergency triple-bypass.
2014	Tricuspid (heart) valve replacement.
2015	Heart stent.
2024	Second heart transplant.

I can't remember the last time the Craig family didn't meet our medical insurance out-of-pocket maximum in the first half of the year. In 2024, we hit it in February. One huge blessing is that my employer at the time of this writing provides excellent medical insurance and has been generous with me.

So how do I do it? How can I go through all of these crappy health experiences and maintain a positive outlook? First and foremost, I am a Christian guy. I have faith that His plan is actually perfect for me. If you're around me enough, you'll hear me say things like "eternal perspective," "in the context of eternity, this is just not that big a deal," or "you need to pick your head up and focus on the big picture." Whether or not you are faith-based, I believe you need something much longer-term to fix your eyes on, especially during rough times. In Berkshire Hathaway's 2024 annual shareholder meeting, Warren Buffett said he thinks about what he wants his tombstone to say and then lives a life that helps make that true. Whatever your perspective is, find what your bigger picture is.

Secondly—and more practically—I have developed the discipline to understand how my experiences shape who I am and to proactively look for ways that terrible experiences can have a positive (or at least neutral) impact on my life.

This starts with dealing with hard experiences head on, without delay. Putting it off until later or just not dealing with it could have a greater impact in the future. I then focus on trying to reframe the impact that difficult experiences have on who I am. Here are three ways I do that:

FLIP THE SCRIPT. Undergoing a second heart transplant is a difficult experience, without a doubt. The surgery is painful, and the recovery is laborious. Because of the transplant, however, I am able to produce the book that people have been encouraging me to write for twenty years *and* live a more robust life because my heart is doing what it should. That's a positive impact.

COUNTERBALANCE THE NEGATIVE. Sometimes negative experiences impact you in ways you can't control. In these moments, I look for positive experiences to help offset the terrible ones.

DON'T INVEST THE ENERGY. Some of those negative experiences have a negative but less meaningful impact. Take my Mohs surgeries, for example, a procedure that removes skin cancer without damaging the healthy skin around the cancerous area. My first dealings with skin cancer in the late 1990s felt significant. Now, I probably have five to ten procedures a year, and they no longer faze me. I don't expend any energy trying to change the impact.

In this book, I write about some of the major influence areas in my life and how I try to balance them to maintain a positive outlook.

INFLUENCE AREAS. For me, the primary influence areas include my health-related experiences, like my two heart transplants and emergency triple-bypass; my relationships; my vocation, including job transitions and everyday work life; and my faith and service.

EXPERIENCES. Each of my influence areas encompasses a wide variety of experiences. I share a number of them—good and bad—to explain how I evaluate their ultimate influence on who I am.

IMPACT. Impact is about how I let experiences affect who I am as a person. Am I going to wallow in self-pity or proactively try to flip the script?

All of these stories are true to the best of my memory. Where the stories involve others, I have reached out to verify details. Writing this book has been a fulfilling experience for me, and I hope you find it valuable.

Getting the Most from This Book

Those who know me well would likely agree that I am a disciplined, outcome-oriented person. One example of that discipline is me staying within a six-pound weight range for the last fifteen years. That desirable outcome has been influenced by the fact that I blew up like a balloon after my first transplant. I never want to get that big again. To remain within my range, I eat the exact same thing for breakfast and for lunch during the week. For breakfast, it's thirty-five squares of Frosted Mini-Wheats and a grape-flavored PowerAde Zero. For lunch, it's turkey, ham, and swiss cheese on bread. My wife says that's not really a sandwich because it doesn't include lettuce, tomato, or condiments. I also have chips of some sort and about 200 calories worth of vanilla-flavored cookies.

If I approach the top of my range, I hold the cheese on my sandwich and eat carrots instead of chips. Because I can keep to that discipline, I will never have to lose ten pounds.

This discipline extends to my understanding of how my experiences shape who I am and how I can generate positive or neutral impact from negative experiences. If I focus on what I can learn from a bad experience or what I can do that I would not otherwise have been able to do because of those bad experiences, that experience becomes more palatable.

I hope this book helps you perform an ongoing self-assessment of the major areas of your life that have been most influential in shaping who you are today. With that, you can evaluate how much of each influence area was influenced by positive, neutral, and negative experiences, and how much of those experiences had a positive, neutral, or negative impact on who you have become. Finally, you can determine how you want that mix to look a year from now and develop goals.

This is a self-assessment, period. You may need someone who is professionally trained to help you through tough times in your life. After my first transplant, I was jacked up on so many steroids to fight rejection that my mind went off the rails. I tried to start a business and buy a car with zero income, and I made hundreds of dollars' worth of long-distance phone calls to launch the business. I saw a psychiatrist for months as I came off the prednisone and became more myself. Seeking professional help is a good move when the emotional water gets too deep.

TAKE
HEART

Section I

Health-Related Experiences

If someone comes up to me and says, "I've got good news and bad news," I am a "give me the bad news first" guy. That's why I'm leading with the area in my life that involves my most difficult experiences. It's also an area that many people might not list as a primary influence on who they are today. Little did I know that what I thought was bronchitis as a sophomore at Vanderbilt would be so influential to what makes me who I am thirty-five years later.

I'll focus on three health-related areas: heart issues, collateral damage, and "I am not a robot." The heart issues top my negatives list. Collateral damage comprises all the health issues related to the effects of anti-rejection medications that suppress my immune system. A suppressed immune system makes me vulnerable to other health issues. Finally, the "I am not a robot" section deals with mental health. I am a pretty stoic guy and don't get fazed by concerns that might upend other people. That comes from thirty-five years worth of encounters with serious health issues. I have, however, navigated mini-breakdowns because I was just weary of having to endure yet another crisis. Having someone there for you during those breakdowns is critical. For me, it's my wife Sandy, who is always here when I reach the end of my rope.

As with each influence area, I share my personal experiences in the detail that I remember them. If the details or stories become too much, feel free to skim and skip. Hopefully, my sharing will provide you with a helpful framework for your own self-reflection.

Chapter 1

Heart Issues

It really is a miracle that I am still here. I honestly could have died a number of times over the past thirty-five years, but, by the grace of God, here I am. My heart journey began in the fall of 1988, when I was a carefree sophomore at Vanderbilt University and the social chairman of Beta Theta Pi. The Betas had just reconstituted the chapter after being kicked off campus several years before. The University had returned the fraternity house to us, so we could start throwing parties again. I had a season full of parties planned, my favorite being "The Cold-Blooded Bash." The Beta mascot is a dragon, and I had hired a local band called the Kingsnakes to perform. What wasn't working out quite as well was my academics. I had a whopping 2.14.

My roommate was the pledge trainer, who, as an Air Force ROTC guy, was in spectacular shape. When he wasn't working out, he would eat an entire loaf of peanut butter and jelly sandwiches. Sometimes I would help him train the pledges, which included going on runs to try to whip them into shape.

In October, I developed a cough that sounded like bronchitis. I had grown up in a healthy family that rarely visited the doctor, so I was well trained to just wait it out. I still tried to help my roommate with the runs, but I was having trouble keeping up with the slowest pledge. Typically, I was one of the most athletic in the fraternity.

The girl I was dating at the time finally convinced me to go to Vanderbilt's Student Health Center to have the cough checked out.

THE SHOCKING DIAGNOSIS AND FIRST TRANSPLANT

Student Health performed bloodwork and found my white blood count was much higher than it should've been, so they decided to order a chest x-ray. The nurse came back with my films, closed the door, and started crying. That was just a little disconcerting. She said, "You have an enlarged heart. It is two and a half times the size it should be." In a daze, I didn't comprehend what that would mean. They scheduled me to see an internist and then a cardiologist, and neither could explain what was happening. The first week of November—my birthday week—they admitted me to the hospital to learn more.

After ordering every test they could think of, the doctors said I had idiopathic cardiomyopathy. They explained that a virus had entered my heart, expanded and weakened it, and then left. I had two options: have them implant a defibrillator to shock my heart if I went into cardiac arrest or go for a heart transplant. Still being in a "this is not going to change my life" mindset, I asked if I'd be able to play contact sports with a defibrillator. The doctors said probably not. I opted for the heart transplant.

Over the next two weeks, they paraded a number of people through my hospital room who were living healthy lives after their transplants. I was unimpressed. They finally said they would have Jimmie come by to see me. He was running marathons. I asked, "Is he winning?"

About two weeks into my hospital stay, I was watching the movie "Running Scared" with Billy Crystal and

Gregory Hines. I felt a little dizzy and closed my eyes. The next thing I know, ten medical professionals were standing over my bed and a crash cart. I had gone into cardiac arrest, and they had to shock me back. Three days later, I went into cardiac arrest while sleeping, and they had to shock me back again. The third time, only a few days later, I knew what it felt like and when it was coming. I grew dizzy and fought to keep my eyes open. That didn't work. I went into cardiac arrest, and they had to shock me back for a third time.

Three heart attacks in one week shot me to the top of the transplant list. The wait was painful. Being a "healthy" twenty-year old stuck in the hospital is no fun, and weeks felt like months. Finally, on December 22, we learned that a heart was available. They prepped me, and I was lying on the operating room table. About fifteen minutes later, one of the doctors entered the OR and said, "This heart isn't going to work." They rolled me back to my room. I felt devastated, convinced that the transplant would never happen.

On Christmas Eve, my family went out to dinner with my girlfriend's family. I had asked them to bring me back a fried shrimp dinner. Around 8 p.m., the doctor came to tell me that they had another heart. I called the restaurant and told my Dad he could hold up on the fried shrimp dinner because I was about to go into the operating room.

After the surgery, I asked what was the fastest someone had been discharged after a transplant. The team said thirteen days. So, twelve days later, I walked out of the hospital because, well, everything is a competition.

"THE LORD'S NOT READY FOR HIM YET"

A few weeks after leaving the hospital, my temperature spiked, so one of my brothers who was staying with me decided we needed to go to the ER. We didn't know that I was in stage 3 rejection, which now means a 20 percent survival rate. Back then, the chances were actually less than that. The doctors honestly thought they had done all they could do. One of the doctors pulled my Mom outside the hospital room and said, "Dave's got 24 hours to live. Why don't you call John (my Dad) and have him come down (from our home in Cincinnati) so he can be here when Dave dies." Being the father of a twenty-year-old and an eighteen-year-old now, I can't imagine how devastated I would be if a doctor told me that. My Mom, who we always joked had a direct connection to God, knew differently. She looked at the doctor and said, "No, the Lord's not ready for him yet." What? The Lord's not ready for him? What are you talking about? My guess is that's what the doctor was asking himself. I'm sure he said something like, "Well, why don't you have John come down just in case."

Dad made the trip, but wouldn't you know I didn't die in 24 hours. In fact, the next week I was still hanging on. The doctor pulled Dad aside and said, "That's one tough SOB in there." The issue then was that I had rejected the heart so badly, they believed I would need another heart transplant, and so the same doctor shared the news with my Mom. I'm sure he was thinking, *What is this lady going to say this time?* Mom did not disappoint. She said "No, he got this one on Christmas Day."

LIVING WITH THE HEART TRANSPLANT

"Recovering" from the rejection was an extremely slow process, and I never got back to where I was physically before knowing I had heart issues. Another problem was that I wasn't a great patient. The medical folks loved having me talk about quality of life, but not so much about following directions. After about five years, the transplant staff at the hospital changed, so I just stopped going. I visited my primary care physician, who had done a cardiology fellowship. I thought that was good enough.

During one primary care visit, my doctor was running through my medications. Prednisone? Yes. Allopurinol? Yes. On it went until he said,"Potassium?" I said no. He looked up at me and asked, "Who told you to stop taking potassium?" I replied, "Nobody. The prescription ran out, and I just never got it refilled." I mean, I'm a smart guy. They had taken me off Lasix, which is a water pill that can deplete your potassium. So if I'm not on Lasix, I didn't think I needed the potassium. Apparently, that was flawed thinking. He said, "Don't you know that if your potassium level gets too low, your heart could just . . . stop?" I said, "I'll get right back on that."

One major test that wasn't happening when I took the primary care route was biopsies and cardiac caths to check for rejection. When I started dating my wife Sandy in 2001 and told her I had a heart transplant, she knew the drill because her dad had a kidney transplant two months before mine. When she found out I wasn't being followed by a transplant team, she was in disbelief. A condition of her marrying me was that I would do what I needed to do from a transplant perspective. She refused to go all in on me if I wasn't going all in on myself. Wise woman.

I had to schedule a cardiac cath for the first time in more than five years. Doctors use two primary heart procedures to test for rejection: a biopsy and a left heart cath. With a biopsy, they go through your neck, and you can pop right up after the procedure. With a left heart cath, they go through your groin and want you to lay flat for 24 hours after—a big difference that I had forgotten about after five years. I walk in the hospital to get my cath done . . . in a suit. The nurses couldn't believe it. I said I planned to go to work after the cath, but I decided to see how the procedure went.

The doctor who was performing the cath procedure was a bit of a wildcard from the nurses' perspective, which was great for me. After he finished, he said, "Everything looks great. See you in five years." That's certainly not what Sandy wanted to hear, but I also saw my opening. I said, "Great, can I go to work now?" He replied, "Sure, if you feel up for it." So off I went to work. About an hour later, as I was slouching down in my chair and feeling very uncomfortable, I called Sandy and asked her to take me home.

"DON'T MOVE YOUR HEAD"

Fast forward ten years. Unfortunately for our family, Mom had Alzheimer's disease and ended up going to her eternal home on October 30, 2012, at the age of seventy-four. Just ten days later, I was riding my LifeCycle exercise bike in the basement and couldn't get through my typical high resistance level. The next day, I had a double's tennis match and told my partner about it. I said that I might need to shut the match down early if I got to be as out of breath as I was the morning before. The good news is that we lost so quickly, I barely even got my heart rate up.

Two days later, though, I couldn't get through the second-highest resistance level and knew something serious was happening. I called the transplant office, told them what was going on, and suggested I needed a cardiac stress test. (Sandy absolutely loves when I diagnose myself and tell the doctors what they should do). The doctors decided I needed a cardiac cath instead. I wasn't a fan of that because I had people to see, places to go, and work to do, so a stress test avoided the required 24-hour downtime. This was another example of me losing the "negotiation" (which was never really a negotiation). Cardiac cath it was, and they were going to squeeze me in four days later.

On Friday, November 16, 2012, Sandy and I drove to Emory/St. Joseph's hospital in Atlanta for my cardiac cath. When we arrived, my name was missing from the schedule. I knew something serious was going on with my heart, so I said that we weren't leaving and that they needed to figure it out. They were able to bring me back just an hour or two after I was originally scheduled.

Cardiac caths include a local anesthetic at the site for the cath, but I told them not to give me any sedation. It probably drives them crazy, but I like to watch the screens and ask the doctors questions during the procedure. This time, I had a pretty good idea that they were going to see something was wrong. As they were winding down the cath, the doctor asked one of the cath lab team about my weight, which I thought was an odd question. I asked, "What's going on guys?" The doctor flipped one of the screens around and pointed to what looked like a little clamp around my left main artery. He said, "You see this? We call this the widowmaker. You're having bypass surgery today, and don't move your head. We don't want your blood flow to change."

For those of you who know me well, you can see how much of a God thing this was. For me to (1) call the doctor because something is wrong and (2) insist that they get me on the schedule when I wasn't on it instead of walking out the door was divine intervention. If I had chosen to do what I would typically do, I wouldn't be here to share the story.

THE GREAT WIDE OPEN

The triple bypass was extremely difficult for the surgeon because of the scar tissue and damage that twenty-five years of immunosuppressants had done. He said that no one should try to open me up again. The problem was that, just nine months after the surgery, I was potentially facing another open-heart surgery. I wasn't recovering like I thought I should. I became short of breath just walking between buildings at work. I called the transplant office, and they decided on a procedure to examine my heart from the back side.

Those who get squeamish should skip this next paragraph.

One of the ways that doctors check for rejection after a transplant is by performing biopsies, where tiny pieces of transplanted organ tissue are evaluated under a microscope. Sometimes, the little clipper can clip the wrong tissue. The tricuspid valve acts as a parachute and keeps blood from backing up into the heart. Sometimes during a biopsy, a doctor will clip the strings of that parachute, making it less effective.

After the procedure, the doctor said that with transplant patients, they typically expect a 1 cm. opening in the tricuspid valve. With me, that opening was 6 cm. My valve was wide open and not doing its job at all.

The next step was to meet with the surgeon who specialized in tricuspid valves. Although he had performed hundreds of tricuspid valve surgeries, he had never tried one with a transplant recipient before. He said that by the time transplant patients were experiencing tricuspid valve issues, they were encountering so many other problems that the tricuspid valve was the least of their problems. With me, the tricuspid valve was the only issue.

He offered three basic options: open my chest up again and replace the valve, replace the valve robotically through my side, or do nothing. Based on guidance from the surgeon who performed my triple bypass, the first option was not realistic, and based on what I wanted for quality of life, the third option was not ideal either. We had to put our chips on option two.

This would be no gimme, though. Replacing the valve robotically through my side with all the scar tissue I had would prove difficult. Interestingly, when placing a new heart, transplant surgeons usually rotate it just a bit. My tricuspid valve surgeon couldn't explain why, but they do. Because my heart was slightly rotated and enlarged due to the now defective valve, the doctor could navigate around the scar tissue and replace the valve. I personally believe this is another example of God, in His divine providence, making all the details work out.

FIRST TIME FOR EVERYTHING

Between 2015 and 2020, my heart situation remained pretty stable. In the fall of 2020, however, I found myself becoming increasingly short of breath. I was scheduled for a cardiac cath in mid-December, but I felt that I needed to accelerate the schedule. I scheduled an appointment with my transplant doctor on November 18 and updated him. He gave two options: keep the cath appointment for mid-December or have him admit me that day and undergo the cath the following day. I chose the latter. That night as I slept in my hospital room, a nurse busted in around 3 a.m. and yelled, "Mr. Craig!" I woke up startled and said, "What?" She left, then returned three minutes later to check my vitals. She asked, "Are you feeling ok?" I said I was fine. She told me that my heart had stopped for ten seconds, which was a complete surprise to me.

They determined that I was in atrial flutter, where the upper chamber beats too quickly and doesn't pump enough blood, which can lead to heart failure. The next day, doctors shocked my heart back to a regular rhythm, but they weren't confident it would stay normal. They also performed the cath and realized that my overall heart function was weakening.

At this point, the primary concern was the irregular heartbeat and deciding whether it should be treated with medication or a pacemaker. For now, they decided to try medication.

During random moments over the next seven months, my Apple Watch would notify me that my heart was racing (130 beats per minute when I was sitting down), but the quickened pulse wasn't affecting how I felt. In June 2021, though, Sandy and I were about to walk our dogs, and I was really out of breath after walking 100 feet. I turned around to walk back toward the house. I let her know I was going to call the transplant emergency line to share what was happening and that they would likely want to admit me. I made the call to the answering service and walked up the stairs to start packing a bag. When I reached the top of the stairs, I was so out of breath and dizzy, I had to immediately sit down. My pulse had dropped to the 40s from my normal rate in the 70s.

Sandy asked if she should call 911. She has been through a ton with me over the past 20+ years but has never asked if she should call 911. She has driven me to the emergency room plenty of times, but she could tell that something was different. I typically downplay dramatic moments, but this time I really wasn't sure that I would make it to the hospital if I wasn't in an ambulance, so I took my third ambulance ride. My first experience was the time I was hit by a car at age ten, but that's a different story.

Once we arrived at the hospital, I told Sandy that the doctor would probably not discharge me without a pacemaker. By the next day, I had one in my chest. That night, I was supposed to meet my boss of nine months in person for the first time because of COVID. That meeting didn't happen.

NOT GOING TO GET THE WORLD RECORD

An internet search for the longest-living heart transplant recipient will display a number of articles about people they claim are the longest living. Why?

Before January 1988, no centralized record-keeping system existed to definitively identify them. From what I've read, it might be a woman in California who received a heart transplant in 1984 when she was two years old. I made it to thirty-five years, three months, and three days with my first heart transplant.

In 2022 I realized my heart was failing when I noticed a continued decline in my ability to complete basic tasks; I struggled to climb a flight of stairs, take the dogs for a walk, or maintain any walking pace. It was another God-nudge that pushed me to ask the doctors to perform a cardiac cath in November. My medical team and I had decided back in 2021 that we would count on echocardiograms every year and cardiac caths every other year to check my heart function since caths are more invasive. When I asked for a cath, my nurse reminded me of our plan. I insisted that we needed to do the cath now.

For educational purposes, ejection fraction (EF) is a value that identifies what percentage of blood in your heart is pumped out with each heartbeat. A normal ejection fraction for an adult is between 50 to 70 percent. In 2019, my EF was on the low side of normal (50 percent), and in 2021 it had dropped to 40 percent. My cath in November 2022 indicated that it had dropped even further to 30 percent. Anything less than 40 percent is a value that concerns doctors, so 30 percent was certainly alarming. After the cath, my current transplant doctor, the cath specialist, and my transplant nurse discussed the results with Sandy and me and had us schedule an appointment for a week later to devise a treatment plan.

I thought that they would tell us that my heart had another five years or so and then I may need another transplant. However, during the follow-up appointment, the doctor said his experience led him to believe the heart might have two years left. TWO YEARS! We were shocked. After dropping that bombshell, he walked over and side-hugged Sandy. This was completely appropriate, but you could tell that hugging patients and family members was not something he usually did. He accurately perceived that his prognosis was much worse than we were expecting.

This estimate meant that my heart could begin to fail when our daughter would be a senior in high school and our son would be a sophomore in college. Our kids have endured so much with my health challenges and their own, but this would likely be the most significant, and at a time when we would just want them to enjoy being teenagers.

The next time we talked, the doctor changed the estimate from "two years" to "within two years." Our next step was to decide on the right place for me to be added to the heart transplant list. The best in the world . . . for me.

GOING BACK TO WHERE IT ALL BEGAN

Now that we realized I needed a heart transplant in the near future, we began to investigate facilities. When my doctor told us I might not be a good candidate for Emory Hospital in Atlanta, I felt a bit offended. I thought I would be a great candidate. I've lived almost thirty-five years with a heart transplant and persevered through a number of other significant medical issues. All that I thought made me a great candidate actually characterized me as a very high-risk candidate. Not every heart transplant center has deep expertise and success with high-risk candidates, including re-transplants.

Being the data guy that I am, I dove into the statistics that I could find. A friend at work challenges me to "find the best in the world" when I am dealing with a medical issue, and this time I planned to do just that. I reviewed *U.S. News & World Report* for cardiology hospital ratings and dug into the data from the

Scientific Registry of Transplant Recipients (SRTR) to analyze heart transplant performance between centers from across the country. My choice came down to Vanderbilt and Duke, with Vanderbilt getting the edge from the data, the proximity to Atlanta, and my familiarity. We also felt a peace that God was leading us back to where it all began and that He would lead us through it this time, too.

In our first meeting with the Vanderbilt team, I felt a bit like a celebrity. I was the 16th heart transplant at Vanderbilt (for my second, I'm Vanderbilt's 1,883rd transplant), and no one there had met anyone who had lived as long as I have post-transplant. They even updated their training to say that they have patients who have lived for 35+ years (old materials listed 30+ years).

When we asked about prospective timing, the nurse practitioner mentioned how bad my left heart cath was and "within two years" became "we need to get you on the transplant list ASAP, and then it will likely take six to nine months once you're on." The accelerated pace was unsettling. We went from thinking in terms of a couple of years to thinking in terms of months.

What I thought would be a fairly uneventful two

weeks of scans, tests, and labwork—a head-to-toe analysis to determine if any little thing might disqualify me—ended up being a highly stressful three months of follow-up scans and tests because of the results. The thirty-five years of immunosuppressant medications had taken their toll on the rest of my body. Fortunately, nothing about the results was serious enough to disqualify me from making the transplant list.

On April 17, as Sandy and I were driving back to Atlanta from Vanderbilt after a clinic appointment, my pre-transplant nurse called to tell us that I had officially been added to the list. I struggled to believe that, after almost thirty-five years, my transplanted heart had taken me just about as far as it could.

THE YEAR-LONG WAIT FOR THE SECOND TRANSPLANT

The wait for the second transplant was a trial. The original estimate was somewhere between six to nine months. At eight months (December 2023), we had our first "dry run," where we drove four hours from Atlanta to Nashville only to find out the available heart wouldn't work. Three days later, Vanderbilt called and said another heart was available. Two hours into our drive, they called back to say it wasn't going to work. In January and February, we made our third and fourth dry runs, where hearts became available but didn't pan out. Finally, on March 27, 2024, the call came about a donor who had been a young, healthy man. We cannot know the details of the donor or how he died, but we are eternally grateful that, in their time of complete devastation, his family chose to donate life.

Through this taxing year-long process, God was present in every detail. My wife reminded me of the time in the book of Exodus when God parted the Red Sea as the Israelites tried to escape from the Egyptians. Exodus 14:12 reads: "And the people of Israel went into the midst of the sea *on dry ground* (emphasis added), the waters being a wall to them on the right side and on the left." If the ground was muddy and wet like it should've been, the Israelites could not have escaped, but God took care of that crucial detail.

With us, the wait and the dry runs were emotionally exhausting. We wanted the transplant ASAP. We were also worried about how all of this was going to disrupt our kids' lives. Our son Owen, then in college at The University of Tennessee-Knoxville, was rightfully worried about how my transplant would impact his performance. Our daughter Julia, then in high school, continued to be overbooked like many teenagers with multiple AP classes, club volleyball, a job, and more. She rarely has a minute to spare, so we were concerned about the transplant's impact on her.

For us, I believe God picked Thursday, March 28, 2024, for the transplant to happen. It was a shock to all of us, but not Him. This was the day of the Last Supper, where Jesus told his disciples that he was going to die and rise again on Easter. Our son was driving home on a Wednesday because the University of Tennessee inexplicably had a two-day break leading up to Easter weekend. We didn't see any other college around us, including SEC schools like the University of Georgia, Auburn University, or the University of Alabama, that had scheduled a break for Easter.

Our daughter's spring break was the week after Easter, so she could spend the first week after my transplant with us without worrying about keeping up with homework. Some may chalk all of this up to coincidence. If you look at the totality of my life, though, this explanation becomes increasingly implausible. I see it all as yet another example of God's perfect plan for me and my family in action.

Chapter 2

Collateral Damage

A transplant of any kind requires a patient to take immunosuppressant medications for the rest of their life to prevent the body from rejecting the transplanted organ. The body will always treat it like a germ. Even after thirty-five years with the first heart transplant, I was still on anti-rejection medications.

When the immune system is suppressed, not only is it preventing the body from rejecting the heart, but it also leaves the patient more susceptible to other health-related issues. In this chapter, I'll write about some of the "collateral damage" I believe the medication caused.

UNDEFEATED

About a year and a half after the first transplant, I was back on the tennis court. I was a decent player before the transplant, so I did my best to return to playing. (I'm looking forward to doing that again after this one—I've been off the tennis court for ten years now). I partnered up with Rob, a fraternity brother, and we entered an intramural doubles tournament.

We won the first match handily and advanced to the next round. Our second-round opponents were considerably better than those we faced in the first round, and we split the first two sets. Going into the third set, I began experiencing severe stomach cramping, to the point where I wasn't sure I'd be able to finish. I was able to power through by relying heavily on Rob, who was much better than me, and we ended up winning 7–6 in the third set.

After the match, I returned home to my apartment and collapsed. The next day, I was supposed to meet Big E (Everett) and Gordo (Gordon) for lunch. Big E called me at 12:30 p.m. to ask me where I was. I was still in bed. The next thing I knew, EMTs were standing over me, attempting to pull me onto a stretcher. Unfortunately for them, I lived on the third floor of a walk-up apartment with a narrow staircase. They navigated me down the stairs and took me for my second ambulance ride.

Once I arrived at the hospital, doctors diagnosed me with ulcerative colitis which necessitated removal of a foot of my colon. The hospital recovery was a week, but they needed to wait a month for the severed sides of the colon to heal so they could reconnect it. During that month, I had to rely on a colostomy—a very embarrassing experience for me (I'll let you look that one up).

If I didn't have friends like Big E and Gordo, my colon would have burst, and who knows what would've happened. The good news is the colon healed as it should have, and I have had no other colon issues since.

100+ MOHS SURGERIES

The next set of "battles" involved skin cancer. Some of my anti-rejection medication makes me particularly susceptible to skin cancer. My first Mohs surgery was in 1997, and it felt like a big deal to me. My skin cancer doctor absolutely loved experimentation and using pigskin grafts to cover cancer spots that he removed. Over subsequent few years, I probably had fifteen to twenty skin cancer spots removed, replaced with nice pigskin grafts. When we moved to

Atlanta in 2006, I found a female skin cancer doctor. She was absolutely fantastic, in part because she actually cared about how a spot looked cosmetically after a procedure. Imagine that.

In 2008, my skin cancer doctor moved her practice too far away, so I found a new female skin cancer doctor. She and I have a close doctor/patient relationship. I can now tell when I have a skin cancer spot. I take a picture, text it to her, and ask if it is something that should concern me. She will usually say yes and have me come in for her physician's assistant to perform a biopsy. She is booked out months in advance but always finds time to squeeze me in.

Increasingly, the skin cancer spots are big enough that they require a skin graft to heal appropriately. I have altered the song "Head, shoulder, knees and toes, knees and toes" to "Head, shoulders, neck, back and thigh, back and thigh." I can feel skin from all of those areas by touching the left side of my face.

THE SKIN CANCER TUMORS

Once again, stellar patient that I am, I stopped going to see my skin cancer doctor for a few years. After a few years, though, I saw that I had swelling in the left side of my face, so I returned to see him. The minute he saw the left side of my face, he said, "That's a tumor." That was not what I wanted to hear. He said he would need to partner with a facial plastic surgeon and an otolaryngologist for the surgery.

The next step was to schedule an appointment with the facial plastic surgeon. He was a no-nonsense guy. As he examined the scans of the tumor, he said, "We'll probably have to cut off the entire ear to take care of this." Sandy said, "His entire ear?" The doctor said, "Would you rather him have some of his ear or for him to be alive for your [then three months-old] son's high school graduation?" Not much bedside manner.

The plan was for the skin cancer doctor to handle the "soft tissue" of the tumor and the facial plastic surgeon and otolaryngologist to address anything that made it to the bone, as well as the reconstruction. What I didn't realize then was that soft tissue was not only surface skin, but all of the tissue between the skin and the bone. I have a bad habit of wanting to see the damage that is being done in the process of Mohs surgery. After the skin cancer surgeon removed all the tumorous soft tissue and was about to bandage my face up, I took a quick look in the mirror and felt a huge pit in my stomach. It looked like a bomb had exploded by the left side of my face.

They bandaged me up and had me prepped for the facial plastic surgeon the next day. Unfortunately, I had arrived with no idea about how significant the soft tissue removal would be. I had actually driven myself to the appointment. Here I was, with my entire head bandaged up like a mummy, and I decided to drive myself home. I can't imagine what that guy sitting next to me at a red light was thinking when he saw me behind the wheel. The next day, Sandy drove me to the surgery, which went as expected. Fortunately, because the surgeon took care of all the soft tissue (and took all day to do it), he only took the part of the ear affected by the tumor. If left to the facial plastic surgeon, I fear he would've just cut the entire ear off.

The recovery was extremely difficult. The surgeon had to transplant significant skin grafts from my thigh and side to replace the skin on my face. He initially said that the best way to help it heal was to leave it open to the air. With a skin graft, they removed the surface level of a 3 by 4 inch section of my thigh skin, leaving all of the nerves under that skin exposed to the air. That was some of the worst pain I have ever experienced. At our follow-up two weeks later, I told him about the excruciating pain of the healing process. He said, "You're leaving it uncovered? You should really put Tegaderm on it. That should make it far less painful." That was frustrating.

The facial plastic surgeon and otolaryngologist couldn't agree on whether I should undergo radiation as a precaution, so I didn't do it. A year later, the tumor came back. This time, our surgeon was one of the best doctors I have ever had. Not only was he expert at what he did, but he was also kind and willing to answer all of Sandy's questions—and she often has many.

He performed the surgery and insisted that I start radiation treatment. I had just taken a job in Atlanta and asked if I could have the surgery in Cincinnati and the radiation in Atlanta. He said not a chance. He wanted to make sure we treated the tumor right this time.

The next appointment was with the doctor who was going to oversee the radiation. He said that the treatment would take six weeks. I asked him if we could do it any faster. I mean, I had a new job waiting for me. He said we could do it in four weeks but that side effects like fatigue would be more severe. I agreed to that. About two weeks later, I was talking with Sandy about how puzzled I was that I was so tired. You can imagine her response.

We moved to Atlanta and began to be followed by a local otolaryngologist. Everything seemed fine for about two years. As I was holding my six-month-old daughter one day, she accidentally headbutted me on the left side of my face, which caused a shooting pain. I scheduled an appointment with the new doctor and discovered that the tumor was back, even after radiation. For a third time, we were going to battle that tumor.

The following year, my daughter headbutted me again, resulting in the same shooting pain. I called my doctor to share that I thought the tumor was back again. It was. Skin cancer tumor surgery #4. Another sequel? Yes, I ended up needing a fifth surgery, and that was the straw that broke the camel's back for me. I write about the emotional impact of that later in the book. Fortunately, I have not needed a sixth, so we can put this one behind us.

I've racked up other collateral damage experiences, but these had the most significant impact on me. In the context of the heart issues and these three collateral damage areas, the rest of my medical challenges haven't been nearly as devastating.

Honorable Mention Collateral Damage: cholecystectomy (gallbladder removal), two primary and one secondary cataract surgery, pneumonia, frequent gout and cellulitis.

Chapter 3

I Am Not a Robot

The Bible verse Romans 8:28 is very meaningful to me: "In all things, God works for the good of those who love Him, who have been called according to His purpose." I think sometimes people misinterpret this verse to mean that they might be spared challenges in life. My experience has been that life can sometimes really suck. In this chapter, I'll talk about how some of these experiences impacted me emotionally at the time and how I reflect on them today.

HITTING THE BOTTOM

Let's return to the first transplant. Even though I didn't die from rejection or need another transplant, keeping me alive just about destroyed both my body and my mind. The next four months were brutal. I was the 16th heart transplant Vanderbilt had ever performed, so no one had much experience in handling my degree of rejection. The doctors ramped up the immunosuppressant medication to keep my immune system from rejecting the heart, and the meds started to work. The issue was the side effects that accompanied those high doses of immunosuppressants. The least serious was that my hair started to fall out. I would wake up in the morning, and my pillowcase would be covered with my hair. The good news is that this was temporary. The more serious impact was that it screwed with my mind (which some of you might think didn't go away, but I promise you, it did).

One of the medications was prednisone, which is still used today to treat a number of medical issues, including transplants. When you are prescribed prednisone up to 100mg per day for weeks, your mind can start to go a little—maybe even a lot—crazy, especially if you are bedridden and have no other outlet to exert energy. My mind was running a mile a minute, and I couldn't slow it down. I literally couldn't close my eyes for any length of time. Back in the late '80s, hospital TVs went blank between midnight and 7 a.m. All you would see was a blue screen with a digital clock in the upper right corner counting the seconds. I would watch that clock . . . all . . . night.

The bigger problem was during the day, when I could actually interact with people. I thought up all kinds of crazy business ideas and tried to recruit people to work for me, including my Vandy fraternity brothers. My dad finally had to ask the hospital staff to disconnect the phone so I couldn't make any more long-distance calls.

The other issue with remaining bedridden for more than four months is that you can't counteract the medication's physical impact, like added weight and muscular atrophy. Prior to the transplant, my weight had dropped to the 140s (which is pretty light for a guy who's 5'11"), but I still had muscle. While fighting the rejection, I had ballooned to over 200 pounds, and all my muscles had atrophied. To move from the hospital bed to a chair, nurses would pick me up and place me in a chair because my leg muscles simply didn't work.

That was both the physical bottom and my emotional rock bottom. As a twenty-something year old, I had always considered myself a pretty good looking guy and a pretty good all-around athlete (OK, Jay, I considered myself a VERY good athlete. Others likely thought I was a "pretty" good athlete). I had now lost that self-perception and needed to face the reality that I may never again be the person that I liked being. Now that I'm in my 50s, I realize what a shallow view I had of myself, but it was real—and painful—to me back then.

FACEPLANT

Although I never considered myself a runner before my first transplant, I did run to stay fit and to enjoy time to myself. My Sony Walkman played a mix tape with songs from INXS, The Hooters, and other great '80s bands during my 3- to 5-mile runs. Sometimes I used this solo time to make big decisions. I still remember going on a run to decide whether to attend Miami (OH), Indiana, or Vanderbilt for college. I came home from the run and told Dad and Mom that I was choosing Vanderbilt. I said it was time for me to challenge myself to reach my potential. Those who know about my time at Vanderbilt know that I worked very hard . . . at being the social chairman of the fraternity. In my pledge class, the person with the lowest GPA was called "bottom of the sea." Unfortunately, that was me.

Just two years after that college decision-making run, I couldn't even walk. That did not last forever, though. I had to start with standing, just getting my legs under me. I slowly progressed to stepping from the bed to the nearby chair. After a few weeks, I was able to walk carefully around the hospital floor, pushing my IV pole beside me.

Although my legs began to work again, my mind was still spinning a mile a minute. One day, as I was strolling around the hospital floor, I thought I heard the phone in my room ring. "Knowing" that it could be a very important call, I turned around and started to run back to my room. What I learned was that just because you can walk around the floor doesn't mean you have the leg muscles needed to run. I took one step to run and faceplanted with my IV pole toppling down with me. I couldn't help but laugh hysterically as I lay on the floor. Adding insult to injury was that it wasn't even my phone ringing.

As my legs grew stronger, my rehab started to include my upper body. From a pride standpoint, this was worse than my faceplant. I could lift about 25 percent of the weight that I was able to lift before the transplant. I felt embarrassed. I am quite sure that not being able to get over my pride impeded my recovery.

What I've learned from that experience and others is articulated well by two great philosophers: my son's orthopedist, who told him to "suck it up, buttercup" when he was complaining about physical therapy, and Denzel Washington, who said, "Dreams without goals are just dreams." I've learned not to focus on what was or could've been, but rather what is and what could be if I put the work in. Life is too short to spend time fixated on the past.

WEARY FROM IT ALL

Ugly crying. That's what my teenage daughter calls it when you sob cry over something. I can think of five times that I've ugly cried as an adult. Two were at the funerals of my grandmother on my Mom's side and my Mom. When I tried to verbalize what those two women meant to me, I couldn't speak the words because I was ugly crying. Once was when I had been working 80 hours a week for four months straight leading the rebranding of seven different brands at the same time. At church, when the worship team sang "Come to Me" by Christian artist Aaron Shust, especially the line, "Come to me, all you who are weary and burdened, and I will give you rest," I sat down and ugly cried. I was certainly weary. The other two times were related to two surgeries—one heart issue and one collateral damage surgery.

The triple-bypass was a particularly awful surgery to recover from, and fourteen months later, I faced the potential that they were going to crack my sternum open again to replace the tricuspid valve. I couldn't imagine having to endure that again only fourteen months later. I still vividly remember returning home from work one day and being greeted by Sandy. The minute she looked at me, she asked, "What's wrong?" I broke down, gave her a big hug, and started sobbing. I said, "I am just tired." I was tired of being stoic. I was tired of having massive surgeries with long recoveries. I just wanted it all to go away.

The next day, I was listening to Aaron Shust's "Come to Me" on the way to work, wallowing in my weariness. I finally thought "forget this" and switched to Building 429's "We Won't Be Shaken." That helped me refocus on moving through this hard time.

The second surgery was related to the skin cancer tumor that I wrote about in the previous *Collateral*

Damage chapter. The tumor had resurfaced for the fourth time, and each time, the surgery crept closer to damaging my entire left eye. The thought of losing my eye devastated me: ugly cry #5.

My experience with the mental health side of negative experiences confirms that a strong support network is critical as I navigate my most negative experiences. The great news for me is that my support network is deep (as you'll read later).

Summary of Health-Related Experiences

I mentioned in the intro to this section that I am the type of guy who likes to hear the bad news first. In my life, health-related experiences have certainly been my "bad news." The key for me has been how to reframe the bad news. That has required two approaches. First, I remember that God has a perfect plan for my life and that all of these "bad things" are part of His plan to make me who He wants me to be. Second, I rely on some of the strategies I discussed in the introduction: flip the script, counterbalance the negative, and don't invest the energy.

My ability to employ these strategies has developed over time. The way I think about my health-related issues and deal with them today, after plenty of reps over the past thirty-five years, is WAY different from the way I felt about them three decades ago. Hopefully, what I've learned the hard way will help someone dealing with faith-shaking challenges for the first time.

HEART ISSUES

None of my heart issues could be considered positive experiences. Most were extremely painful and required long recovery times. The ablation, stent, and pacemaker were more neutral experiences, but none were positive. From an impact standpoint, I wasn't equipped during some of those early heart procedures to think about how negative experiences could have a positive impact at the time. I've developed that discipline as I have matured and continued to encounter health challenges.

The good news is that now that I have the strategies, I can reflect on all of my life experiences. The most negative physical experiences—the two transplants and the triple bypass—allowed me to continue living, to build a great family with a wonderful wife and kids, to have a great career, and to be able to serve others well. Without those surgeries, I wouldn't be alive for any of it. That's a complete flip of the script.

COLLATERAL DAMAGE

The colon and skin cancer tumor surgeries were extremely tough experiences with mostly negative impact. The skin cancer tumor surgeries were the first time people could outwardly see that I had a significant health issue. I rarely take my shirt off outside the house, so people don't see the scars from heart surgeries or the damage done by the skin cancer procedures. Out of the 100+ Mohs surgeries, probably twenty-five to thirty of them rose to the level of negative experiences that had an impact on who I am.

With the most severe of the skin cancer surgeries, my strategy was to counterbalance the negative, to focus on positive facets of my life, like relationships, career, and service. For the more minor skin cancer surgeries, my strategy was to not invest the energy in self-pity.

LOOKING AHEAD

The problem with my health-related experiences is that they are completely unpredictable. I simply have no idea when or how often they will happen, so I can't plan for them. My main strategy is to remember I've been there before, and I will move through them just like I have before.

The great news is that the bad news section in this book is over. My health has been a regular challenge over my life, but it has certainly helped build my character. Over the next few sections, I'll discuss three other critical areas that have helped me counterbalance the negatives of my health experiences.

Section II

Relationships

Many people likely identify relationships as a primary influence on who they are, in good or bad ways. At the height of COVID and the years following, relationships have suffered for many. In May 2023, the U.S. Surgeon General declared "loneliness" a public health epidemic, and a poll by the American Psychiatric Association in early 2024 found that 30 percent of adults have had feelings of loneliness at least once a week within the previous year.

I have counterbalanced the negative impact of health-related issues and maintained hope because of strong relationships I have developed over the years.

Sandy and I have collectively connected with hundreds of people over the course of our lives who we call friends. Some we actively engaged with for shorter periods or less deeply than others, but they all played important roles in making us who we are today. I believe the key is intentionally nurturing existing relationships and building new ones. As challenging as my health-related issues have been over the past thirty-five years, hundreds of old and new friends have traveled alongside us to provide support and prayer when we've needed it most. It would have been very, very difficult for us to endure what we've experienced without our families and this caring network of friends.

I think of relationships in terms of type (lifelong and season-of-life) and category (family, community, mentors). Every relationship involves at least one type and one category.

The relationship categories are pretty straightforward. Community is a broad category that could include the people in your neighborhood, workplace, school, place of worship, etc. The relationship types need a bit more description:

Lifelong: These are the relationships where you are really *doing* life with someone. You intentionally connect deeply with them, and they step up to support you in your most difficult times. You can be your authentic self, never needing to worry about changing who you are to be accepted.

Season-of-Life: These relationships form during a specific moment in life. They could be school-related, like high school and college friends, or friendships with the parents of your kids' friends during seasons of their lives. These relationships may fade once that particular season passes.

I believe it's important to value relationships in all these areas, with a caveat for season-of-life relationships. As I described above, with lifelong relationships, the important thing is that you can be who you are today without fear of acceptance. You can reminisce about the past and even poke fun at who you were in the past before you grew into who you are today. Season-of-life relationships run a risk of not just reminiscing but actually reliving the past and being transported back to who you were in the past. I have seen that happen at several high school class reunions. I do not particularly like who I was in high school and have zero interest in reliving it. I have seen others revert back to who they were, which is fascinating to watch.

In the next few chapters, I'll share some of the key relationships that have significantly influenced who I am today.

Chapter 4

Family

PARENTS

My family has been a primary influence. I grew up in what was a fairly traditional Christian family in the 1970s and 1980s. My Dad was the "breadwinner" and my Mom was the "homemaker." I have six brothers and sisters, and we lived a stereotypical middle-class life.

Mom was a strong Christian woman who spent her life helping others see the Jesus that she knew and loved. She would meet with each of us kids for an individual Bible study each week and have us underline verses that talked about God's promises in green and our responsibilities in red. She led women's Bible studies at our church. She would visit the inner city each week and go door-to-door praying for people living there. She would spend a month a year in Africa helping at an orphanage by serving the kids meals, reading to them, and leading them in various activities. I believe Mom was the greatest influence on my heart for giving back.

With Dad, I think about hard work, achievement, and sacrifice. Where Mom primarily focused on our spiritual development, Dad focused on providing us with the opportunity to be successful in whatever career field we chose. Education was important to him. He told us early on that we could go to whatever college we thought best, but we had to pay a third of the cost. That meant he and Mom would have to pay two-thirds of college expenses—for all seven kids. To do that, he partnered with a friend to operate a franchise for a tune-up business, in addition to his nine-to-five corporate job. He worked at the franchise every Tuesday and Thursday night and all day on Saturday. I believe Dad has been the greatest influence on my work ethic and my drive to achieve.

Despite their busy schedules, my parents invested in each of us individually. Mom would take us each on "days out" to a spot of our choosing (Frisch's Big Boy for me) to enjoy a little dessert and spend time chatting. Dad took us each on "nights out," usually to dinner (Roy Rogers restaurant for me) and then to a movie or mini-golf. As I remember those times, I marvel at how consistently they engaged with each of us individually.

My parents aligned in terms of discipline, and they were strict. Clear boundaries were established, and the only thing we kids needed to think about was if we could deal with the consequences if caught. Most times the answer was a painful yes. Corporal punishment was alive and well in the Craig family when I was a kid. In fact, Mom got so tired of the brothers bickering and tattling on each other, she introduced the "Tattle Paddle." The rule was that the brother who told on another brother would get half the swats as the one who actually got ratted out. This significantly reduced the tattling but didn't eliminate it. As the youngest brother who got pounded on frequently, I sometimes thought half the swats were worth it so my big brothers would suffer a consequence.

My parents were also different. Although they very much loved each other, they had different interests. Dad liked going to New York City to see

Broadway plays and eat at five-star restaurants. Mom liked to spend her time praying for people in the inner city and volunteering at an African orphanage. Once we kids were all adults, Dad would have "family meetings" to update us about him and Mom. One time he began to say, "If your Mother and I die together . . . " I interrupted and said, "Dad, the only way you and Mom would die together is if this condo blows up. You never do anything together."

SIBLINGS

My siblings have also helped shape who I am. From an early age, we were forced to share life together. For about six years, our parents and four of us boys lived in a five-bedroom house. Because Mom and Dad wanted us to learn to share, Scott and Doug (the oldest two) shared a room, Bill and I shared a room, and we had two guest rooms which were rarely used (until Katherine came along—she enjoyed her own room for a while). Sharon and Dorothy eventually came along, and nine of us occupied a five-bedroom house with no guest rooms to spare.

Although we fought and bickered growing up, nothing was ever a relationship killer. We are now in our mid-40s to early 60s and genuinely enjoy spending time together and watching our kids interact. Although we live in four different states, we make a point of gathering for a long weekend in the summer and every other Christmas.

With my second transplant, each of my siblings (and spouses) helped by either staying with me in Nashville following surgery or staying with our daughter Julia in Atlanta as I recovered. I have been blessed to have so many siblings and actually relate well to all of them. The spouses—Vicky (Doug), Kristine (Bill), Sandy (me) and Joe (Dorothy)—have been gracious enough to deal with all of the Craig idiosyncrasies.

Each of my siblings has also been successful in our respective career fields: two investment professionals, a general contractor, a pastor, a teacher, a nurse practitioner, and a left-brained marketer (me). We were all fortunate to be born into a family that valued education and had the resources to send us all to college. After we became adults, Dad and Mom decided to give back the money we had contributed to our college expenses, explaining that it was the idea of "skin in the game" that they were trying to instill in us.

WIFE AND KIDS

In December 2000, I was working at the Economics Center at the University of Cincinnati and about to start my self-created, full-time MBA program, which I planned to complete while working full-time. I happened to run into a friend who, as part of our conversation, asked if I was dating anyone. She had a good friend named Sandy and thought she would be a good match for me. I was game, so we made a plan.

We decided to initiate a blind date, actually a double-date with my friend and her husband. We went to Zip's Café in Cincinnati's Mt. Lookout neighborhood and then went bowling—what I call the great equalizer. The outing went great, and Sandy and I started dating. I didn't have a ton of time to date, but we made it work. A few months into our dating relationship, she asked, "Why can't we ever be spontaneous?" I said, "We can be as spontaneous as you want—between 8 and 10 p.m. on Tuesday or Thursday nights." She was an absolute champ through all that schedule madness, and we married the month after I completed my MBA.

Sandy learned early on that my health would produce bumps in the road. Returning from our honeymoon in the northwest (Seattle, Vancouver, Whistler), my leg had blown up like a balloon, and I was having trouble walking through the airport. When we arrived home, we saw a doctor. He asked two questions: "Have you been eating any rich food or shellfish?" and "Are you under any unusual stress?" On our honeymoon we had steak and seafood for most dinners, so the answer to the first question was a resounding "yes." To the second question about stress, I answered "no." Sandy was stunned. She told the doctor that we had just gotten married, I was starting a new job, and we were moving into our new house—all in a thirty-day time-span. Maybe I was a little bit stressed after all. They diagnosed me with a severe case of gout and cellulitis. Each was painful by itself, but the compound effect was excruciating. Fortunately, healing didn't take too long, but this was the start of the bumpy health journey that Sandy and I have navigated together.

Now that we were married, one of our first orders of business was to find community as a couple. Both of us had great friend groups that we had developed individually over the years, but we also wanted a group of friends that we developed together. We found that in spades with a group called Dunamis at Montgomery Community Church in Cincinnati. This group of thirty to thirty-five couples in their mid-20s to mid-30s was led by Vance and Mindy McLarren, who are still mentors of ours over two decades later. I'll share more about this group in the *Community* chapter and more about Vance and Mindy in the *Mentors* chapter.

After a year-and-a-half of marriage, we decided to start a family. I had more than a decade's worth of immunosuppressant meds that I thought might be working against me, and Sandy's parents had a difficult time conceiving her, so we weren't sure we'd be able to have biological children. We were willing to adopt if we couldn't. We asked my Mom to pray for us, and four months later, we found out that Sandy was pregnant. We had just returned from an Ireland vacation where we had a reasonable amount of Irish beer. We jokingly apologize to our son Owen to this day that his mom was saucing it up in Ireland while she was pregnant with him.

Almost two years later, I took a job in Atlanta. We drove away from Cincinnati on July 7—Sandy's birthday and the middle of summer—leaving our home, neighborhood, friends, and family that we loved and moving to the face of the sun (Atlanta) while Sandy was six months pregnant with Julia. This was 2006, right when the housing market shut down. For the first eight months in Atlanta, we paid on two mortgages since it took much longer than expected for our Cincinnati house to sell.

The next eighteen years were filled with the fun times and the growing pains of living as a family of four in suburban Atlanta. We are still in a great neighborhood with lots of families, public schools that have been wonderful for our kids, a church that challenges us to grow in our faith, and a wide range of sports opportunities for our kids. We've enjoyed watching our children at their various sports and activities and struggled when it's taken six hours on a Saturday to motivate strong-willed kids to complete a twenty-minute chore. As they say, "The days are long, but the years are short." I continually pray that I will be a good husband to Sandy and a good father to Owen and Julia, imperfect though I am. Looking back, I'd do some things differently, but I only think about past mistakes if I can make better choices moving forward. Dwelling on the past does me no good.

As we were "doing life" in north Atlanta, our family experienced a huge shock to the system during the second year of COVID. When I had my transplant, the doctors attributed it to "idiopathic cardiomyopathy." A random virus entered my heart, expanded it, weakened it, and then left. Our pediatrician had been telling us we should measure a heart baseline for the kids, but given that my heart issues were caused by a random virus, we didn't think that was urgent. A nurse friend of Sandy's told her that COVID was affecting kids' hearts. Given the pediatrician's recommendation and this new information about COVID, we decided to schedule a doctor's visit for the kids.

The appointment was such a non-event to us that I didn't even go. In fact, I did not even realize Sandy and the kids were at the appointment when I saw that Sandy was calling me. I picked up, and Sandy said the doctor had a question for me. He asked what caused my need for a heart transplant. I replied that it was idiopathic cardiomyopathy. I told the doctor that I had my transplant in 1988, and he said, "Those were the dark ages. We didn't know anything about anything back then. It appears that both of your kids have early signs of cardiomyopathy."

Stunned. It just can't be, I thought. My heart issues were caused by a random virus. The next step was to take the kids to consult with pediatric heart failure doctors. They performed gene testing and found a gene called RBM20 that both weakens the heart and causes arrhythmia (irregular heartbeat). Someone carrying that gene has a 50 percent chance of passing it on to their kids. For us, it was 100 percent because both kids had it.

At the second appointment with these doctors, I was on day ten of battling COVID, so I couldn't join them. Owen was supposed to pitch in his high school baseball game that night, so I drove down to the building's parking lot to take him to his game. When Sandy told the nurse that, the nurse said, "I'm sorry, but I think the doctors are going to shut both of them down from competitive sports until we have a better understanding of what this is." We couldn't believe it. At that point, Owen had one love—baseball—and that was being taken away. Julia had a wider range of interests but was very disappointed to be sidelined from playing volleyball.

After several months of tests, the doctors became more comfortable with Owen and Julia participating in competitive sports, with some limitations—no sprinting, no squats, and no heavy weightlifting. For Owen, that meant he would be a pitcher only for the rest of his baseball career. For Julia, it meant that she could not participate in all the volleyball team's conditioning drills, which is hard when your teammates think you're just trying to avoid the hard stuff. Some even said they wanted to trade places with her. Julia would've taken that trade in a second.

The next step was treatment. Both kids were in the early stages of cardiomyopathy. Owen was beginning to show signs of reduced heart function and arrhythmia. Julia was just showing signs of reduced heart function. Both were prescribed a slew of medicines to stabilize the heart and prevent it from growing weaker. For Owen, the doctor recommended an "implantable cardioverter defibrillator" (ICD). The device would be implanted on his left side and would shock his heart back to a normal rhythm if he were to go into cardiac arrest. We couldn't believe we were talking about Owen going into cardiac arrest, but we certainly wanted that safety net. At our next appointment, the doctor said he'd been researching the RBM20 gene and had learned that people who had the gene but didn't have arrhythmia had gone into cardiac arrest. With that information, we decided to go the ICD route with Julia as well.

A few years past the diagnosis, our kids were continuing to figure out how best to live with the disease. Owen didn't get to live out his dream of playing college baseball, but he was able to thrive as a Vol at the University of Tennessee. Julia switched from volleyball to cross country and really loved the team. Well, she loved her teammates, she just doesn't really love the running part.

The family I have—parents, siblings, wife, and kids—makes it hard not to feel optimistic. To know that I have them with me through health crises and through unexpected life events gives me a peace that is not easy to explain.

Chapter 5

Community

As I mentioned in the section introduction, Sandy and I have been extremely fortunate when it comes to the friendships we've developed over the years. I have great friends that go back more than forty years and some that have been an active part of my life for only a handful of years. All of them have played important roles in my life, whether that role has continued over the course of my life or at specific points of my life.

In this chapter, I'll highlight some of the friendships that proved critical at special moments.

CINCY BOYS (AND WIVES)

This is my core group of lifelong friends and their spouses who I've known for more than three decades—Bill & Holly, Ted & Robyn, Jason & Natalie, and Greg & Shellby. We became friends through our high school and early college years. They have supported me and my family through all of our ups and downs, and we have been present for each other through marriages, kids, kids' marriages, and now increasingly through our parents' health issues and deaths.

After family, these four guys are the first people I text when something is going on with me and my family.

VANDY FRATERNITY BROTHERS

My Beta Theta Pi fraternity brothers at Vanderbilt played two very important roles for me. The first was creating a sense of belonging. In high school, I always felt on the edge of a few different groups of friends, but I didn't feel like I had a core friend group that was mine. My Vandy fraternity brothers—especially my pledge brothers—became my first core friend group. The eleven of us in my pledge class all came from different cities and had different backgrounds. The pledging experience united us and had us working together.

The second role was as a support network after I was diagnosed with cardiomyopathy. I lived four hours away from home and didn't know anyone in Nashville. These guys were there for me before the surgery and during the excruciating recovery. I've lost touch with many of them over the years but have reconnected with a few of them as I write this book.

CHPC SUMMER STAFF

In the summer of 1989, I returned to Cincinnati as I continued to recover from the significant rejection from the transplant. Because the medication had caused massive weight gain, people I had known for years literally no longer recognized me.

Sibyl (mentor #1) had given me a job working on my church's summer staff for day camp and resident camps. Some on the summer staff I had known for years, and some I was meeting for the first time.

The staff spent hours together during and outside of camp. This group fully accepted me for who I was, which I very much needed at this time in my life when my insecurity was sky-high.

Interestingly, three of my four CincyBoy friends

married women who were part of that summer staff (Jason married Natalie, Ted married Robyn, and Greg married Shellby).

UC FRATERNITY BROTHERS

In the fall of 1989, my original plan was to complete a year at the University of Cincinnati while my heart issues stabilized and then transfer back to Vanderbilt the following year. Although I didn't tell anybody, I knew at that point that I was not returning to Vanderbilt. I was too embarrassed to go back, given how crazy the meds made me right after the transplant and my heavier appearance.

On the first Friday night of the quarter, I remember sitting in my apartment watching TV and feeling incredibly lonely. All my summer staff friends had returned to their normal lives, and my apartment mate Roger—one of my best friends in middle school and high school—was at work. I decided that this loneliness wasn't OK with me and committed to visiting the Beta house the next day to introduce myself to the fraternity brothers.

When I walked in the Beta house, I ran into Stu and Alan. One of them was wearing an Ohio State football jersey with the #25 on it. That was Carlos

Snow's number. Carlos and I had grown up in the same neighborhood, and he would frequent the deli where I worked in high school. That jersey put me at ease from the very beginning, and Stu and Alan became good friends of mine through college. With the Cincy Betas, I now had an immediate family that was critical for me during my UC years.

DUNAMIS

Dunamis was the young couples group at Montgomery Community Church in Cincinnati that Sandy and I joined shortly after we married in 2002. The group of thirty to thirty-five young married couples was led by a couple named Vance and Mindy. When we joined, only two couples had children, and Vance and Mindy was one of them. This group combined Sunday morning "Sunday School," weekly small group Bible studies, and plenty of social activities. We were really doing life together with a number of these couples.

In our second year with the group, twenty-one of the couples became parents, and two years later, nineteen couples either added a child or had their first. The beauty of this is that we were all friends, and now our kids could become friends, too.

This group was also very important as I went through the first skin cancer tumor surgery that destroyed the left side of my face. Group members stepped up with meals, prayer, and anything else we needed. This was our first friend group that we developed mutually as a couple, and a number of them remain great friends to this day.

ATLANTA FRIENDS

In 2006, Sandy and I left Cincinnati for Atlanta for my new job. Owen was nineteen months old, and Sandy was seven months pregnant with Julia. Out of the four million people in Atlanta at the time, we knew four—two couples from Dunamis had moved to Atlanta in 2005 and early 2006. Both couples lived more than thirty minutes away from us, so we were effectively starting over. Although this was hard given the tight network we had relied on in Cincinnati, the move was right from a career standpoint.

We started building friends through our neighborhood, our kids' school activities, and the church we have been attending for almost two decades. Many of our core Atlanta friendships are with couples we met within a year of moving to Atlanta.

The key for me and Sandy with these community

friendships was initiative and intentionality. We had to put ourselves out there, which felt uncomfortable at times but proved well worth it.

Chapter 6

Mentors and Coaches

I have been blessed beyond measure with mentors and coaches, both personally and professionally. Some of my mentors had similar personalities as me, but they had more experience and could coach me to develop my given strengths. Others' differences helped broaden my perspective.

SIBYL

Sibyl is perhaps the most influential mentor I have had outside my family. She was the mastermind behind our church's successful summer camp programs from the 1970s through 1990s. She has a gift for seeing the giftedness in others and helping them reach their potential, especially with children and young adults. Four specific stories stand out when I think of Sibyl.

The summer after my freshman year at Vanderbilt, I took a job selling Cutco knives (the best knives in the world—I still have my demonstration set from more than thirty-five years ago, and we use them every day). I demonstrated the knives for Sibyl at church during summer camp, and she bought one. Afterward, she said, "David, you will be successful at whatever you choose to do, and you will be able to make plenty of money. You have a gift of working with young people and teaching, though. I'd like you to consider that." I was a young man motivated to make money, however, so that was never going to happen, or so I thought. Eight years later, I left my business job, earned a certificate to teach high school math, and taught in the inner city for almost four years.

The second story was the next summer, after my first transplant. Because of the impact of rejection, my self-confidence was in the toilet. Sibyl realized that I needed direction and community. She had already hired a woman named Susan as director of the summer camp for 1st through 6th grades, but she offered me the chance to serve as co-director. I accepted. I'm sure my decision surprised Susan, but she handled it with grace. We had a great summer working together and remain good friends to this day. What could have been a season-of-life friendship became a lifelong friendship.

The third story involves our end-of-summer performance review. Sibyl and I both loved watching tennis, so we'd conduct the review while we watched the finals of the Western & Southern Open in Mason, OH. We had enjoyed the summer, and, as always, I'd taken some initiative to shake traditions up a bit. One of Sibyl's main camp themes was to create a "safe place" for both campers and counselors. At our week-long overnight camp, I decided I would throw a little surprise for everyone. While the campers sat on the deck and faced the lodge for singing, I had my co-counselor Tuffer paddle me out to the middle of the lake behind the lodge. I started yelling that I was being kidnapped. All the kids jumped up and ran to the lake as Tuffer conceded defeat on the kidnapping attempt. I wore a life jacket with a shirt over it. At our review, Sibyl said, "About the canoe . . . " I said, "Sibyl, it was a safe place. I had a life jacket on." She said, "Yes, but the kids could not see that." That was a lesson to me that sometimes it's as important to clearly show activities are safe in addition to them actually being safe.

The final story occurred in the middle of the next summer, when I was working again at the camp. I received a call to interview for a marketing internship at a global technology company, working in the Latin America, Middle East, and Africa marketing department. It was a sweet position. I told Sibyl about the opportunity and tried to think of creative ways I could do both, which was an unrealistic idea. She said, "David, I am not going to say no, but you have made a commitment to us." I traveled to Dayton, OH, from Cincinnati for the interview, and it went well. Afterwards, I thought about what Sibyl said. The next day, I called the recruiter and removed my name from consideration. A month later, after camp was over, the tech company called me for a different internship, which I interviewed for and accepted. Doing what was right paid off in spades for me because I had a great boss, and I saw how overloaded the woman who took the first internship was. Interestingly, the manager of the other intern told her that she wished she could have hired me. God spared me on that one.

I cannot thank Sibyl enough for the influence she has had on who I am today.

JUDITH

Judy has played two primary roles for me in our forty-year relationship. For the first five years, when I was a teenager, she was "the humbler." A number of times, she brought me down from my stratospheric self-confidence (OK, I was cocky). One summer, we gathered for the end-of-camp staff party at the Clippards'. They had a tennis court, and I thought I was a pretty good tennis player. Bill Clippard and I decided to take on Judy and her partner-in-crime Sibyl. We were two strapping teenage boys going up against two "old" ladies in their 40s. You guessed it: they defeated us and took the wind out of our sails.

Over the past thirty-five years, Judy has played the more important role of "encourager." Several years after that humbling tennis experience, Judy was diagnosed with primary lateral sclerosis, and I had to have a heart transplant. Two years later, I had a foot of my colon removed, and a year later, I had my gallbladder removed. At that point, Judy realized that I didn't need a humbler anymore. I needed an encourager, so she gifted me the book *Glorious Intruder* by Joni Eareckson Tada.

Judy's life had been drastically changed, and she knew mine was too. Over the last thirty-five years, we have shared with each other how our lives are being disrupted and how God is guiding us. We know that "these light and momentary troubles are achieving for us an eternal glory that far outweighs them all" (2 Corinthians 4:17). This paragraph from *Glorious Intruder* sums Judy up to a tee:

> *Not everyone can be trusted with suffering. Not everyone can endure a fiery ordeal. So the master scrutinizes the jewels and chooses those which can bear the refining, the branches which can stand the knife. It is given for some to preach, for others to work, for others to give and for still others to suffer.*

I thank Judy that God could trust her to suffer and be an encouragement to all who connect with her—whether that's by sending a note to friends who are going through tough times or letting them know she's praying for them.

RIC & JENNY

Ric is one of Sibyl's sons and about six years older than me. He was a tremendous role model when I was in junior high and high school. He is a smart, athletic, and good-looking guy with a large network of friends who love Jesus. He was my camp counselor in those years and someone I always admired.

After high school, he earned a bachelor's degree in mechanical engineering from Purdue University and met Jenny, his lovely and witty wife of more than thirty-five years. After Sandy and I became engaged in 2001, we sought a mentor couple to share their experiences and help us understand what to anticipate.

Ric and Jenny were the first couple that came to mind. We ran into them at a church event and asked if they would be our mentor couple, and they graciously agreed.

We met with them monthly during our engagement. We studied a recommended book together and listened as they shared about their marriage experience. They were completely vulnerable when they talked, sharing about both the good times and the challenging times. Their counsel was invaluable as Sandy and I prepared for our marriage.

During one meeting, we talked about the number of kids we wanted. Sandy is an only child who had dreams of a big family, and I am one of seven who had dreams of a smaller family. Sandy wanted four kids, and I wanted two. Jenny said, "Well, you have to have two to get to four, and at that point, you may be thinking very differently." Her wisdom and humor was valuable to us both.

Ric coached me on loving Sandy well and thinking of how best to serve and support her. He told me about times when he thought he did that well and times when he could've done a better job. That vulnerability was instructive, especially since I can often "lose the people in the process" (Sandy's accurate assessment of my tendencies).

They continued to mentor us for a few years after we married and still lived in Cincinnati. When our son was about two years old I remember Sandy telling Jenny that he had entered the whining stage. Without missing a beat, Jenny, a mother of three teenagers then, said, "Yeah, that only lasts about eighteen years." Funny woman, that Jenny.

VANCE & MINDY

While Sandy and I were engaged, we began to look for a church that would fit us. We found that at Montgomery Community Church (MCC) in suburban Cincinnati. After we married, we joined the young married couples group led by Vance and Mindy. They had recently moved to Cincinnati from Indianapolis, where they had been leading a similar group. The

MCC group had already grown to about thirty couples by the time we joined. Sandy and I became involved with Sunday morning meetings, social activities, and a weekly small group of six couples that Vance and Mindy facilitated.

They were a half a stage of life ahead of us, and their guidance in our marriage and when we became parents was invaluable. I still remember Mindy's coaching as we had our first baby when it came to getting him on a good sleep schedule early so that we weren't exhausted all the time.

Twenty years later, we still keep in touch with them and even had a chance to visit with them several weeks after my second transplant. Their passion for serving and mentoring others has truly influenced our lives.

RON

A number of my bosses have become lifelong friends, and Ron is one of them. He supervised me at the Economics Center in the early 2000s. His Student Enterprise Program helped Seattle-area students learn about economics and entrepreneurship. He replicated the program in New Zealand and then launched it in the Cincinnati area out of the University of Cincinnati. He was full of passion and operated with a "how can we do it" attitude rather than a "why we can't do it" mindset.

As an introvert, brainstorming can sometimes be frustrating for me. When I come up with ideas, I also assess the viability of the idea before I mention it. If I know the idea can't be executed, why even mention it? Ron had the gift of being full of ideas, but also practical. His ideas could actually work. We would spend hours talking about possibilities and then determine which ones made the most sense to advance.

JULIA

Julia is a mutual fund product development and administration expert. She is confident in her expertise and also knows areas when she needs someone else's expertise, like marketing. When she offered me a marketing director role, she expected me to bring the expertise, whatever that looked like. I came in to overhaul just about everything. Quarterly communications about investment performance of mutual funds is a standard practice for mutual fund families, and the best fund families have these available by the 15th of the month following the end of the quarter. When I entered the scene, the team was struggling to distribute them even after thirty days. The vendor they had been working with handled a range of services for Julia, and she had a tight relationship with them, but when it came to these quarterly communications, they were too slow and too expensive. I told Julia I had a better solution: ddm marketing & communications (ddm), a marketing agency I had worked with from Grand Rapids, MI. I assured her I could contract with them to produce these statements in half the time for less than half the expense. Julia was all in and handled the political implications of that change. Julia empowered me multiple times to make decisions and then helped smooth the way from a political standpoint when necessary. Her confidence in me helped bolster my confidence in myself.

JIM

In our first official meeting with him as my boss, I told Jim that I didn't agree with the decision for me to report to him. He was not surprised. I also acknowledged that he was good to his people and that my team and I were now part of his people. Finally, I explained the way I work: I would fight hard for my ideas behind closed doors, but if I couldn't convince him, I would execute whatever he decided, whether or not I agreed. Jim's perspective was that we had a small sales team, small marketing team, small budget, and BIG sales goals. If we weren't making the most effective use of our limited resources, we would not accomplish our goals.

Over the three years I reported to him, we had close alignment and far surpassed the sales goals. Some of our innovative ideas for growing sales are covered later in the book.

RILLA

Rilla is the first career-related mentor I had who I didn't have a direct working relationship with, and she was fantastic. I had taken the job of marketing director for the mutual fund family of a large southeastern firm. I reported up through the investment management business, so I was the top marketing guy and had no one to answer to from a marketing perspective. I had met Rilla through the interview process. She was leading marketing for the Private & Institutional Wealth Management businesses of the overall company and reported to the chief marketing officer.

After I started in my new role, I asked if she'd be willing to meet for monthly breakfasts so I could bounce ideas off of her and hear her perspective. She was more than willing. We'd talk about the work she was doing, which helped broaden my perspective, as well as the work that occupied me. She asked incisive questions that targeted the "why" of my choices as well as the potential long-term benefits. She helped me think about more than just the next quarterly campaign.

I ended up accepting a position that reported to Rilla almost seven years later when she was chief marketing officer and had a great year-and-a-half working with her before she took a big role leading a different business area.

BARBARA

Barbara was my first-ever executive coach. To improve the effectiveness of the marketing leadership team at my large southeastern firm, Rilla brought Barbara in to help. Barbara would attend all of our team meetings and conduct one-on-one sessions to discuss our own personal development as well as how she thought we could best add value to the overall team based on her observations.

In our individual sessions, we covered not only business relationships, but also personal ones. She provided insights on how I could best relate to Sandy and avoid counterproductive choices. Her biggest impact was in helping me relate to one of my peers, someone who frustrated me because his ideas were polar opposite to mine. I just didn't understand it. She pulled out our Myers-Briggs assessments and said, "You are both thinkers, but in everything else, you are different. You need to understand that as you interact with him." From that point on, I figured out how to better relate to my colleague and reduce my frustration.

SUSAN

Susan was my boss for six years, my longest-tenured boss over my thirty-year career. Susan was hired to take Rilla's position as the new chief marketing officer. I was still trying to get my footing in the B2B Marketing Director role, but Susan exuded confidence in her role. I wondered if I would measure up.

I had reached a point where I felt I was having to "fake it until I make it." I considered myself a smart guy with good ideas, but sometimes I wasn't sure if my ideas would actually work. My *modus operandi* was to speak with confidence, and if no one pushed back, off we'd go. Was she going to see that I was just making stuff up as I went along?

Susan showed the same confidence in me that she demonstrated in herself. When I had doubts, she helped me see potential landmines to consider but ultimately entrusted me with decisions once she was sure I had all the relevant information.

When I transitioned from the B2B Marketing Director role to the Marketing Strategy & Operations role, she completely trusted me to run the business side of marketing. I worked with Finance and Sourcing to ensure that we had the budget and vendors we needed to operate and also helped articulate the impact that marketing was having on the business. Susan's strength was creating an inspiring brand that was attractive to our target audience. She was more than happy to delegate the logistical side of marketing to me.

VINOO

Vinoo was the third Chief Marketing Officer that I reported to at the southeastern firm, and all my same insecurities surfaced. Is this new guy going to bring in his own team? Is he going to see the value in what I do? Over the previous eight years, I believed I had added value to the marketing team, but I felt less able to clearly articulate how. I was the guy who worked in the background to keep the train on the tracks. I was the fixer who stepped in when problems arose. For the previous CMO, I was charged with "the business of marketing," like dealing with finance, procurement, legal, and other departments, so that she could remain focused on creating the most compelling brand. In my initial assessment of Vinoo, I felt that he liked the business of marketing, so I became insecure about my spot.

In one of my early meetings with Vinoo, I shared this perception with him. I described my work for the previous CMO and voiced the concern that he may no longer need me in that role. He shared that he was interested in *knowing* what was going on with marketing, but he had no interest in *doing* it. He would still need me for that. He also said he would need me to help transform the marketing organization into one that was hyper-focused on driving revenue using modern marketing strategies, with a heavy focus on digital and more relevant use of our own client data. He initially wanted me to lead that transformation, but we both realized that I didn't have the relevant experience for that. And rather than try to get me up to speed, it made sense to bring in a highly experienced outsider to accelerate the efforts. His decision proved wise.

Vinoo not only leveraged my problem-solving strengths, but also broadened my knowledge of modern marketing techniques, for which I am very appreciative.

Summary
of Relationships

Each category (family, community, mentors and coaches) and type (lifelong, season-of-life) of relationship has been formative in my life. I have been fortunate in that the relationships with family—which I cannot choose—are positive and strong. I know many others who navigate challenging relationships within their families.

In the other categories and types of relationships, intentionality is key. Good friendships rarely come from remaining passive. Sandy and I have intentionally put ourselves out there in different circles: our neighborhood, school, work, and church communities.

The benefit of a broad range of friendships across different categories and types is that, when you are going through challenging times and are willing to share them with people, you will be amazed at how many current and past friends rally to support you. These relationships are extremely helpful as I try to counterbalance my negative health-related experiences.

Section III

Career

My career has been challenging and rewarding. I have managed teams for nearly twenty years, and I always tell my team that if they can't get up every day and say "There's no place I'd rather work and nothing I would rather do," then they need to find a better-fitting role somewhere else. Life is too short to be stuck at a company or in a role that you don't enjoy. A caveat here: all jobs include parts that are a slog, but if that slog overwhelms your satisfaction for a decent period, you may want to start looking. Some days I'd rather be on vacation, but since I have to work, I have been lucky to land in positions that motivate and satisfy me.

I have also been blessed with good bosses across the board—from Mr. Smith to Ron to Rick to Julia to Jim to Rilla to Susan to Vinoo to Sparkle—over the course of a nearly thirty-year career. I have learned from each of them, and they have all let me play to my strengths of innovation and solving complex problems. I would not be a good production line manager if everything was running smoothly. I like to shake things up and experiment with ideas that can help drive success for my workplace. Each of my bosses has provided me freedom to identify opportunities and to seize them. Through it all, though, I remember Colossians 3:23: "Whatever you do, work at it with all your heart, as working for the Lord, not human masters."

I've broken this next section into three primary areas: major career transitions, my time teaching in the inner-city, and everyday work across my different jobs. I'll write about the career choices I've made from financial advisor to inner-city middle school math teacher to financial literacy program manager for teachers to mutual fund copywriter to B2B marketing Director to Marketing Strategy and

Performance Director. I'll also reflect on those jobs I wanted but didn't land, as well as some of the cool ideas I pulled off with my teams.

Chapter 7

Career Transitions
. . . and Not

Because I enjoy novelty, my career features frequent role changes with a maximum of six years and
an average of three to four years in each position
throughout my nearly thirty-year career. This chapter takes a specific look at those changes and how I
believe God was at work in each of the transitions.

PAXTON FINANCIAL GROUP

When I was graduating from the University of
Cincinnati, I had a chip on my shoulder during job interviews. I had come to UC from Vanderbilt, where I
had a 2.14 GPA in the full year that I was able to take

classes, thanks to my focus on being the best frater- nity social chairman I could be. UC wasn't sure I had the chops to succeed in the business program. Well, I showed them and graduated with a 3.9 GPA. As I'm sure you know, that "I showed them" attitude doesn't translate well in job interviews. I didn't receive a sin- gle offer from my campus interviews, so I began scan- ning classified ads in the newspaper.

Remember: this was 1992. I found a posting for a financial advisor at Paxton Financial Group, the agen- cy for a major midwest life insurance company that had an office in the Cincinnati area. I didn't dream of selling life insurance, so I focused on investments and disability insurance because of my health history. This was not an ideal job for me—commission with a draw—but it was employment in what was called the jobless recovery of 1991–1992. After three years of making very little money, I returned to study ed- ucation and to earn a certificate to teach high school math, just like Sibyl had suggested.

INNER-CITY CINCINNATI MIDDLE SCHOOL

I interviewed with a few school districts in the Cincinnati area—one affluent suburban district, one less affluent suburban district, and Cincinnati Public

Schools, which is an urban district. During my interview with the affluent district, the math department head asked me a ton of questions about how I would handle a parent who tried to intervene to influence their child's grade. I'm not very good at hypotheticals, so I held tight to "the student's performance needs to match the grade they get—no exceptions." Apparently, that wasn't the answer she was looking for, so I didn't get an offer there. I'm not sure why, but I wasn't offered a position at the less affluent district either. CPS came through with a middle school math position at an inner-city middle school in the west end, right around the corner from the Police District One building. That will be important to know for the next chapter.

After three years, I decided to leave before I killed someone or someone killed me (kidding). In reality, the majority of my students were good kids from tough environments. This was definitely one of my hardest jobs. Although I think I was a positive male role model, I was not a transformational teacher who could accelerate my students' math achievement after years of "social promotion," where age, not content mastery, drove advancement.

ECONOMICS CENTER/MBA

I was ready to return to the business world, so I decided to go after my MBA. Because I needed health insurance, I looked for a job with benefits that would offer the flexibility for me to earn my MBA at the same time. I actually considered working the early morning shift at UPS.

I continued my search and sent a resume to my undergraduate marketing professor, who was now the Dean of the Lindner College of Business at the University of Cincinnati. He forwarded it to the folks at the Economics Center, a non-profit associated with UC that promotes economics instruction. They were seeking a financial literacy program coordinator who would primarily manage The Stock Market Game, an educational stock market simulation offered online by the Securities Industry Foundation for Economic Education. My time as a financial advisor and as a classroom teacher gave me the perfect background for this role. They offered me the job at the same rate as my teaching salary and allowed me to earn my MBA for just the taxes on the program cost. I couldn't have asked for a better scenario.

A few months later, I attended a Bengals game with a family friend I affectionately call Dr. J. He was a finance professor at UC who started an investment advisory firm from his home that now manages more than $15 billion in assets and serves clients from around the world. I was complaining that it would take three years to complete the part-time MBA program. He asked, "Why don't you create your own program?" I couldn't believe that was an option, but it was. I ended up combining two part-time programs—the evening and the weekend programs—creating a customized full-time program and finishing in a year-and-a-half, all while working full-time.

MIDWESTERN FINANCIAL SERVICES FIRM WITH MUTUAL FUND FAMILY

In the last semester of my MBA program, I began actively looking for a new opportunity. In one of my earlier classes, the professor had us anonymously write down the percent raise we predicted our new degree might generate. Most people landed in the 10 to 30 percent range. I wrote 70 percent, since I was transitioning from teaching and non-profit work into the corporate world.

Trying to hit that 70 percent certainly wasn't a layup. I saw an opportunity for a marketing manager role in the Corporate Marketing Department of a Cincinnati-headquartered financial services firm. I interviewed in the second round with a panel. Two weeks of radio silence passed, then I was called about a role as a mutual fund marketing copywriter. Two of the people on the initial interview panel had forwarded my resume to the mutual fund marketing director (Rick), who needed a copywriter. I showed him presentations and newsletters I had created, and a week later, I received an offer with a salary 65 percent larger than what I made at the Economics Center.

SOUTHEASTERN FIRM WITH MUTUAL FUND FAMILY

After a solid but unremarkable body of work at the midwestern financial services firm, I decided to spread my wings. As 2005 ended, I told my wife that I wanted to be in a new role by the end of 2006, and that probably meant moving to a new city. Cincinnati simply didn't offer a ton of mutual fund marketing roles. We ruled out New York, Boston, Chicago, and anywhere in California and decided we'd move east, west, or south of Cincinnati. That was a limiting decision since many mutual fund companies are based in the cities we ruled out.

One day during a search on monster.com, I found

an institutional wealth marketing manager role at a large firm in the southeast. I had never heard of the company because it didn't have a presence in the midwest. I clicked on the company's website to apply directly and also saw a role for a mutual fund marketing director for the company's proprietary mutual fund family. It looked like a perfect fit, so I applied for that position, too.

The next day, the recruiter for the mutual fund Marketing Director sent me an email to schedule a screening call. He liked what he learned about my background during the interview and set up a phone interview with Julia, the hiring manager and President of the mutual fund family. The next day, the wealth marketing role recruiter emailed me about a screening call and scheduled a phone interview with Rilla, who was the Wealth Marketing Director.

I felt good about those interviews, and the mutual fund marketing recruiter called me later that day to set up in-person interviews. Several days later, the institutional wealth marketing recruiter called me to set up in-person interviews for that role. I told her that I was already coming down for interviews for the other role and asked if she'd be able to coordinate her interviews with the others.

The two days of interviews went well, and I expected at least one offer out of the two. After returning to Cincinnati, both recruiters called me together and said, "Here is the offer. Which job do you want?" I thought, "This is not how this works. They are supposed to tell me which job I got." Both Julia and Rilla were highly accomplished and would be excellent bosses. The deciding factor was that, with the mutual fund role, I knew exactly how I could help. With the institutional wealth marketing role, Rilla explained that they were looking for the data to help them make marketing decisions. That seemed like a risky proposition to move my family to Atlanta for a job in which finding the data needed for success wasn't guaranteed. I chose the mutual fund marketing role instead. Interestingly, the institutional wealth marketing role was eliminated a little over a year later in a round of job reductions.

I was now the top marketing guy for the mutual fund family and would have ultimate decision-making authority from a marketing perspective. Julia was a mutual fund product expert and great boss, but not a marketer, so I reached out to Rilla and asked her to mentor me because I needed to learn from her experience. She agreed, and we met for monthly breakfasts for the next two years, a critical factor in my growth as a marketer.

GETTING LAYERED—TAKE 1

Getting layered happens when your role moves one or more levels further away from the CEO. After two great years reporting to Julia, the Head of Sales was promoted to Head of Distribution, and the marketing function (my team) was rolled under him. I got layered. I looked at this as a demotion, even though Jim (Head of Distribution) was way more experienced than me and had a history of building large, successful sales and marketing teams. I fell into a funk for about a week. Then I decided to go for it: I built an ambitious marketing plan for the upcoming year. I actually included more than I thought we could do because I imagined Jim would push back on some of it. He didn't. I was shocked. I realized that Jim didn't want to micromanage marketing. He just wanted to ensure complete alignment between the sales and marketing plans and teams.

Until this moment, I had trusted God for my health-related experiences, but I thought I could handle career decisions on my own. Getting layered made me realize that His plan for me includes everything.

MOVING TO THE MOTHERSHIP—CORPORATE MARKETING

In 2012, I knew that the parent company was actively trying to sell the asset manager to another asset manager or a private equity firm. I imagined that, if that happened, our headquarters would move to one of our larger offices in New Jersey. I had zero interest in moving to New Jersey, so I started looking.

At the asset manager, I engaged minimally with the parent company's marketing folks. We were a separate brand, and I reported up through the asset manager's leadership, not the parent company's marketing team. As I was completing an expense report one day, I decided to look at what was going on in Rilla's world, who was now the chief marketing officer. I noticed that the woman who led B2B Marketing and reported to Rilla was no longer listed in the organizational chart, and a replacement role now reported to the Head of Brand and Consumer Marketing. I emailed Rilla and said, "If you're willing to have the B2B Marketing Director role report directly to you, I'd be interested in a conversation. Would you?" She said, "Absolutely."

After several rounds of interviews, I was offered the job in October 2012 with a start date of December 1, 2012. If you read the *Heart Issues* chapter, the triple-bypass I discussed happened on November 16, 2012. That delayed my start by five weeks. I checked in with Rilla as I was writing this book, and she said, "I mentored you so that I could eventually get you to accept a job on my team. And playing the long game worked out well for me!"

Play the long game: what a great leadership lesson.

TRANSITIONING TO A STRATEGY AND OPERATIONS ROLE

In 2017 during my annual review with Susan, who was the southeastern firm's CMO at the time, I said, "I think I'm about done with this role. I've done everything I set out to do and just maintaining what we're doing isn't that interesting to me." She said, "You're not done because you don't have a clear successor." "Fair enough," I said, and I spent the next year investing in my team to develop a successor.

A year later, a peer of mine named Stan took the role of president of the company's foundation. The marketing leadership team gathered as Susan and Stan shared the news. Susan then said, "So what are some thoughts on filling Stan's role?" After a bit of silence, I leaned in and said, "What about me?" This falls in the "be careful what you ask for" category. I landed the job, but because I didn't have a clear successor, we had to rely on an internal and external executive search. I ended up working in both roles for six months. This ended up being a valuable career-broadening experience.

GETTING LAYERED—TAKE 2

During a reorganization from top to bottom, the Chief Marketing Officer role was eliminated and Marketing, Client Experience, and Digital were consolidated under the Head of Digital executive. Two of my eight colleagues became direct reports of this new leader, five colleagues became direct reports of the first two, and I was moved under Sparkle, who played a very similar role for the Head of Digital as I did for the chief marketing officer. One major difference between Sparkle and me is that she has deep expertise within the digital space, and I'm more of a utility player who works to solve complex problems.

Just eighteen months before this, I had told my boss that I thought I had about eighteen months to two years left in marketing before I needed to find a different group where I could keep solving big problems and learning. This reorg isn't how I pictured it, but I'm exactly where I said I wanted to be, and Sparkle is a fantastic manager and leader.

THE "NOT" OF CAREER TRANSITIONS

I have interviewed for plenty of roles that I didn't land. The two that impacted me most were rejections by Procter & Gamble (P&G) for a role in the finance area and by T. Rowe Price for a marketing role in their third-party distribution team.

With P&G, I made it to the final interview stage and felt hopeful. I really liked P&G's commitment to their employees' career progression. Every three or four years, they would move you to a different role, sometimes to a different city. That seemed like a great opportunity for someone like me. After receiving the rejection letter, I reached out to the hiring panel for feedback. One of them graciously shared that they saw from my resume that I had jumped around to a number of roles that were significantly different than the roles I had before. With this job, the work was basically the same, but for different brands. In hindsight, I bet a thirty-year career in finance would've bored the socks off of me.

T. Rowe Price was my dream company. I thought it was to asset management what Procter & Gamble was to consumer packaged goods: highly respected, quality products, and great at developing their employees. I made the mistake of checking my email about the position while Sandy and I were on a nice date, heading from dinner to a Broadway series play. Reading that I had gotten dinged soured my mood for the rest of the night.

Reflecting on the last thirty years, I see all the times where what I really wanted at a specific time actually might not have been best for me long-term. I have enjoyed a fulfilling career so far, even though it is not how I would've drawn it up.

Chapter 8

Teaching
in the Inner City

Most readers of this book who have kids will likely be happy with their kids' educational experience because they intentionally moved to a neighborhood with good public schools, decided to send their kids to a private school, or decided to try some version of home-schooling. You have choices, and public schools may have been the best option for you.

What you often hear in the news, however, is a consistently negative story about how American students are falling behind, teachers' unions are driving unreasonable demands, and bad teachers remain employed despite sometimes egregious offenses. All these issues are most extreme in urban environments and are part of the story, but they aren't the whole story.

MY SCHOOL'S ENVIRONMENT

The seventh- and eighth-grade middle school where I taught was located in the heart of the West End in downtown Cincinnati, right around the corner from District One Police Headquarters. The school building was built in 1915 and did not have air conditioning, which made it uncomfortable at the August start of the school year. The student population was about 95 percent African American and 5 percent White, with nearly 100 percent qualifying for free or reduced lunch. The students were organized in two teams of 100, with five teachers responsible for specific subjects for each team. My initial teacher team included a strong (but kind of lone wolf) team leader, two well-meaning veteran teachers who lacked strong classroom management, and two first-year teachers (including myself).

At the end of each class in my first year, we would line up the students and walk them to their next class to minimize—but not eliminate—hallway fights between classes. Four of my team's teachers had classrooms located on the same hallway, so transitioning between those classes was generally uneventful. One classroom, however, was down one floor, so accompanying students down the stairs could be dicey as a different class passed on the way up. I quickly found that when it came to "fights," the boys tended to be posers. They would put their fists up and act ready to fight, but I could gently push one away from the other and end the encounter. Girls, on the other hand, meant business. They punched, kicked, and pulled hair. I usually wore a suit to school with a white shirt. A number of times, my shirt would be smeared with hair gel from breaking up a fight. In my second and third years, we decided to have the kids remain in the same classroom all day and rotate teachers.

MY FELLOW TEACHERS

Each of my fellow teachers cared about our students, wanted the best for them, and worked hard to help them succeed. Like any organization, individual teacher's effectiveness varied, but everyone tried. The student body's range of interests, motivation, and foundational learning also varied widely (which I'll cover in the next section).

The biggest problem our team faced was that no one was well-connected within the school. The other team's teachers were not only friends, but they were well-connected. The summer before my first year, the other team of teachers gathered to review student profiles and hand-select some of the better students for their team. It was like a two-team draft with one team getting both picks for the first twenty rounds. Our team ended up comprised of the most challenging students at an already challenging school.

In my second year, our strong team leader moved to a different team and was replaced by a new teacher. Our team was now comprised of two veteran teachers with weak classroom management and minimal respect from students, two second-year teachers, and one first-year teacher. One issue I have with the education system is the heavy emphasis on tenure and education level over effectiveness. The foregone conclusion was that a veteran teacher with a PhD would lead the team. I was not OK with that. Because of her poor classroom management, she would often send the majority of her students out of her classroom to sit in other classes. By the time class was over, I'd see seven or eight students walk out of her class. I felt like she was tutoring more than teaching, so I led a bit of a coup. I went to the principal and said that it was a disaster waiting to happen if our students could walk over our team leader. He agreed. In our first formal meeting, the teacher with the PhD began to lead the team, and the principal walked in and said, "I'd like David to be team leader this year." I felt a little uncomfortable for about a week, but the others settled in and were able to recoup some sense of control.

MY STUDENTS

The vast majority of my students were good kids growing up in tough environments. Some of my students lived in one-bedroom apartments with eight other people, and some were the primary caregivers for younger siblings as their moms (primarily) worked multiple jobs to try to make ends meet. When you're concerned about where your next meal is coming from or whether you're going to be evicted from your home, traditional school subjects just don't feel like a priority. I did my best to engage them and make math interesting to them, but I knew I had headwinds to overcome.

Some of my students made life harder on themselves. Minor drug dealers would occasionally show up to school, and a number of girls were pregnant at thirteen and fourteen years old. These girls often had mothers who had them at thirteeen or fourteen years old. That means I had twenty-six and twenty-seven year olds who were *grandparents* when they showed up for parent-teacher conferences.

To demonstrate my naivete at the beginning, I was in the office when the secretary said that a student was coming in to see his P.O. I couldn't understand why a student would need a purchase order. The secretary laughed at me a little as she explained it was his parole officer, not uncommon for a number of my students. One day, one of my minor drug dealers showed up to school, and I saw his parole officer later that day. She asked if he was in school that day. I confirmed that he was, and she said "Good, because his mother would rather him be out selling drugs." These students sometimes dealt with more than just financial struggles. The adults in their lives weren't always helping them succeed.

One of my friends got an up-close and personal look at my students when she visited to discuss interview skills. Holly managed a local staffing agency. When she arrived, I took her to the office to check in. The smell of marijuana was pungent. She said, "I didn't think I'd have to talk about drug tests with the students." When she told the students that, one student said, "Yeah, you need to start that at the elementary school." As she moved into interview skills, she decided to roleplay with one of the students. She picked a sweet-looking girl to be the first interview candidate. Holly started by asking questions that were not legal to ask and was going to then explain why, if they are asked those questions in a real interview, they were not obligated to answer. She started with some basic get-to-know you questions before asking, "Have you ever been arrested?" Fully expecting a "no," Holly was shocked when she heard the girl say "yes." Holly followed with, "Why were you arrested?" The girl answered, "I hit a police officer." Holly was floored. This girl did not look like someone who would hit a police officer. Holly gathered herself and said, "OK, well that's not a question that an employer can ask. They can ask if you've been convicted of a crime, but they cannot ask if you've been arrested." It was an educational day for Holly, and just another day in my inner-city teaching experience.

We would occasionally host teacher candidates from a local university for a two-week urban teaching experience. These candidates were as naive as I was and thought that the problem with urban schools was the teachers. They believed that they themselves could be totally successful. I tried to set expectations for them. I would say, "I know that you each believe that you will be able to reach all of the students if you taught here. Consider it a success if you just reach one in each class." The visitors would dismiss my advice and think they could reach everyone. During the first day, everything would go perfectly. Students would seem attentive and create few classroom management issues. At the end of the day, the future teachers would feel justified in their belief that they could outdo us.

On the second day, however, the students would go into action. They had spent the first day figuring out what the best buttons would be to push for each of the teaching candidates, and they would push away on day two. At the end of the day, the candidates would say, "Mr. Craig, you were right!" I said, "I know, but you'll be just fine. Just reset your expectations a bit. Try to reach one each class, and if you reach more than that, that's a bonus."

NEVER LET THEM SEE YOU SWEAT

Going back to one of my lessons from Sibyl in the *Mentors & Coaches* chapter, I wanted to create a "safe place" in an environment that didn't always feel safe for all students. I wanted to convey to my students from the beginning that teaching is a professional job that I take seriously, I mean business, and I'm in charge.

To demonstrate professionalism, I wore a suit and tie Monday through Thursday and allowed myself to wear business casual on Fridays. I would arrive at 7 a.m. when the school day started at 9:15 a.m. and leave between 6 and 7 p.m. when the school day ended at 3:30 p.m. I used the first hour of the day for prep and would let students come into my room to hang out or complete homework before the entry bell. After school, students would generally stay until after 4 p.m. for tutoring help.

During my first quarter of teaching, students quickly realized that I wasn't going to tolerate any crap and that I wasn't going to let anyone disrupt the learning experience for others. I started the year by saying, "Some people might have told you that there's no such thing as a dumb question. I'm here to tell you they are wrong. If I tell the class what page we're on, and you don't hear me because you were talking and then ask what page we're on, that's a dumb question. You should've been listening. If I tell the class what it's supposed to be working on, and you aren't paying attention and ask what you're supposed to be doing, that's a dumb question. You should've been paying attention."

The students weren't quite sure how to react.

In the middle of my first year, one of my sweet female students who sat in the front row asked, "Mr. Craig, do you ever smile?" I looked back at her and said with a deadpan expression, "Yeah, I smile." Another student laughed out loud and said, "I've seen him laughing in detention." OK, she caught me.

In a number of instances, students tried to push the boundaries and test my "I mean business" approach. I realized in my first year that these middle school students lacked some of the foundational math knowledge from their elementary years. At the beginning of my second year, I started the students with multiplication table tests. In one class, I told the students to clear their desks, and I would hand out the test. One student, who had failed the previous year, was back to re-take my class. He wanted to establish himself as the cool kid in class who could ignore the teacher. He left his folder on his desk and stared at me. I said, "Kevin, get your folder off your desk." He just stared at me. I repeated, "Kevin, get your folder off your desk or I'm throwing it out the window." My classroom was on the second floor. He held up his folder and said, "I dare you." Never one to pass up a good dare, I walked over, took his folder, and walked to the window, asking myself if I should I really do this. My answer was "yes," and I dropped his folder out the window. Kevin yelled, "Mr Craig, you're crazy!" I then said, "You know, I don't want that to be a temptation to anyone else, so I'm going to close these windows." I got a big groan from the rest of the class, since it was August and the building wasn't air-conditioned. I didn't have any issues with students clearing their desks after this.

I did, however, continue to encounter students who wanted to test authority. One of my rules was you couldn't put your head down on your desk. In one class, a student decided that he was going to do what he wanted. This student, one of my minor drug dealers who happened to be about 6'2" and 190 pounds, had little respect for any authority. He had his head down in class, and when I said "Montel, get your head up," he ignored me. I repeated, "Montel, get your head up." He ignored me again. I said, "Montel, get your head up or I'm going to call security." He picked his head up, looked at me, said, "Call security," and returned his head to his desk, so I called security. Our security officer arrived and said, "Montel, come with me." Montel didn't respond, so he said, "If you don't come with me, I'm going to get the principal."

Montel said, "Get the principal." The principal arrived to remove Montel, but he once again refused to move. The principal said, "If you don't come with me, I'm going to have the police come to get you." Montel replied, "Call the police." Fifteen minutes later, a police officer entered the room, put Montel in handcuffs, and escorted him out. It seemed like such a trivial thing, but if the other students saw that some students could ignore authority without consequences, they would not have felt safe.

Even though I was a math teacher, I would sometimes help my students with vocabulary. On one day, I was doing something that displeased one of the male students. He yelled, "Mr. Craig, you're racist!" I was floored, as were the other students in the class. I said, "I'm racist?" He said, "Yes!" I asked, "What do you mean?" He said, "You favor the girls over the boys." I let out a huge breath and said, "Oh, that's sexist. I might be sexist, but I'm not racist."

Another time involved one of my rowdier classes when students had trouble calming down toward the beginning of the school year when we were still getting used to each other—and getting used to the steamy school in the August heat. I warned the students that if they couldn't quiet down, I would close the windows to avoid disrupting other classes. The class didn't respond, so I followed through and closed the windows. Kenya yelled out, "Mr. Craig, this is child neglect." I paused for a minute and said, "It's not child neglect because I'm right here with you. It might be child abuse, but not child neglect." That was a joke, of course—it wasn't either.

Even though I didn't let the students see me sweat, I certainly had good and bad days. To pick my head up a little bit, I started tracking whether I thought I won the day or whether I thought the students won the day. I knew I would lose some days, but my goal was to never lose a whole week. I'm happy to say that, although I went into some Fridays with a 2–2 record and needed to secure Friday to win the week, I never lost a week.

INTRODUCING EIGHTH PERIOD

In my first year, as we were approaching the fourth quarter, I knew that the majority of my students were on track to fail the class. I had to think creatively to support those students who would actually try their best to pass. Our school day was divided into seven periods. I introduced what I called eighth period, an extra class at the end of the day where I would cover some of the standards from earlier in the year that students needed to master.

In a controversial move, I ranked all of my students from 1 to 100 based on how many standards they had already passed and posted the rankings on the classroom wall. I told the students that those students who had the fewest number of standards left to pass would get priority in eighth period. If they had been doing the work all year and just needed to pass a few standards, they had a much better chance of passing the year. For those students who hadn't been doing the work all year, this would be more difficult. I had twenty-five desks in my room. I told the students that those were reserved for the highest-ranked students who showed up. I explained that if a student ranked 23 came in and a student ranked 72 was in a seat, the lower-ranked student would have to give up the seat. I was running a meritocracy based on effort and progress, which these students hadn't seen before.

The end result was that double the number of students passed than were passing at the end of the third quarter. Unfortunately, more than half of them still failed the class.

GOING TO CALI

Although some parts of math are about memorizing, like multiplication tables, I did my best to make my lessons engaging to students so they wanted to learn. Two examples were my "Going to Cali" and "Casino Night" units.

In "Going to Cali," I announced to students that we would go to California on Friday and that we needed to learn different ways to calculate the trip's costs. We learned to calculate the cost of gas using gas mileage, gas prices, taxes and fees for hotel rooms, food cost, etc. On Friday, I came in dressed as a surfer with a wakeboard and asked the students to work in groups to calculate the cost. Unfortunately, I sold the idea too well, and some students actually thought we were making the trip to California.

The "Casino Night" unit supported the standards around probability. I taught the elements of probability all week, and then on Friday, I set up my room like a casino. My high school-aged sisters actually had the day off and came dressed in black pants, white shirts, and black bowties to serve as card dealers. Students would rotate to different stations and learn how probability was related to each of the different card games.

Both lessons were highly engaging to the students. Unfortunately, my efforts didn't translate into long-term retention or mastery.

FAILING EARLY

In my first year as team leader, I expanded my focus from how students could succeed in my math class to how they could succeed overall. As we approached the fourth quarter, I identified students who were failing all five of their core classes. Some of them could find the motivation to pull it out, but the odds weren't good. More than likely, they would try to pass every class and fall short in each of them.

I floated an idea with the team. "What if we tell the students right now that they've failed certain classes for the year so they can focus on passing fewer classes and then take the others in summer school?" Trying to pass all five in summer school was also unlikely. I felt that we needed to help them focus their efforts. Three of the teachers strongly opposed the idea because they worried the kids would bounce off the walls in their classrooms. The other teacher, who was new to teaching but had more life experience and teenage kids, agreed with the plan. We decided to tell the kids they failed our two classes and had the other teachers provide catch-up work for students to complete during our class periods. The plan resulted in 30 percent of those students passing a couple of classes so that they didn't face retaking all five classes in summer school.

MEASURING SUCCESS

I failed . . . again (see the upcoming *Everyday Work* chapter for my first failure). I assessed my three-year teaching performance using my perspective as an early-30s driven business guy to determine that I had failed at my job. Over the three years, I was a positive male role model, I created a safe place for students, and I helped a number of them progress to the next level, but I was still failing more than two-thirds of my students. The school paid me to be a math teacher, and my verdict was that I had not been successful. Remember movies like "Stand and Deliver" and "Lean on Me," where a teacher and a principal were able to make dramatic changes that helped their students' success? That wasn't me, so I left teaching to earn my MBA and return to the business world.

Chapter 9

Everyday Work

I have gotten to work on some cool stuff over the course of my career, despite my health-related issues (thanks again to great bosses). Because I was so engaged by my work, I could remain optimistic even when my health took a bad turn. I had plenty to look forward to in my different work roles.

Sometimes it was as an individual contributor, and other times, I led great teams. Occasionally, I made missteps that resulted in self-inflicted wounds, but, overall, the accomplishments outweighed the missteps. In this chapter, I reminisce about some of the projects that most engaged me and helped buoy my optimism in the face of challenging health issues.

PAXTON FINANCIAL GROUP

It's tough to be a financial advisor straight out of college who makes money primarily through life insurance sales. Many young financial advisors work through friends and family and then fade out within the first two years. I was determined to employ a strategy that extended beyond family and friends. I decided to use my health issues to work myself in as a financial advisor who specialized in the medical field, starting with resident physicians.

I created a program called "Fiscal Fitness" and even had "Fiscal" on the custom license plate of my 1986 Mazda RX7 (a Porsche look alike I was gifted by my grandmother). I developed a newsletter and seminars to deliver in a hospital at lunchtime. I would contact the chief resident at hospitals and coordinate a time to present the seminar. When you offer residents free food, they typically show up. The problem was that I was competing against pharmaceutical sales reps whose bigger budgets provided nicer catered lunches for the residents. I had no budget, so I would spend the morning making fajitas at home, buy sides at the grocery store, and set out the meal right before seminar time.

I generated a decent number of appointments from those lunchtime seminars, but what I realized was that resident physicians were a great *long-term opportunity*, but a terrible short-term opportunity if you are commission-based. I learned the ins and outs of student loans very well, which didn't make me any money at all but proved helpful for the residents. In my first two years as a financial advisor, I earned about $20,000 and lived in my parents' basement. This was probably my first career failure. The positive impact, though, is that my Fiscal Fitness seminars were similar to seminars that the midwestern financial services firm wanted to create. I was able to leverage those to land the mutual fund copywriting job.

While I worked as a financial advisor, I also coached junior varsity girls tennis at a suburban high school. Many of the girls worked with private coaches, so my primary role was to teach doubles strategy and to drive the van to away matches. Over my three years as the coach, the team went 59–3 and never lost to the same school twice. This really wasn't due to my coaching prowess. I just lucked into a school where tennis talent was deep.

I enjoyed coaching and decided to explore teaching. I asked the principal what subjects were in demand. He said math or science. I asked about teaching business or economics. He reiterated that math and science were the best ways to go. I am not a science guy, so I picked math. I left Paxton Financial and went back to school to earn my high school math teaching certificate.

MUTUAL FUND FAMILY OF SOUTHEASTERN FIRM

As I mentioned in the Career Transitions chapter, my four years at the midwestern financial services firm was solid but unremarkable. I was engaged more with sales support than traditional marketing, and the majority of projects were assigned to me, not self-initiated. This was appropriate, though, since the position was my first time working full-time in a corporate environment. I needed to learn the ropes.

When I moved to the southeastern firm, I came up with big ideas to improve sales team support that were more marketing-oriented. First, however, I needed to help our salespeople stand on equal ground with our competitors' salespeople. Before I arrived, portfolio managers were encouraged to tell the "best story" each quarter, whether or not the fund performed well. The portfolio managers would share a positive spin. I explained that the "best story" is the "full story" and that we should include what went well and why certain areas had underperformed. That transparency, along with ensuring that quarterly information was available in an industry-standard timeframe, helped our salespeople to grow more competitive and to schedule meetings with advisors closer to quarter-end.

The next step was to develop marketing programs to benefit the mutual fund family and the sales team. My boss Julia always looked at the annual STAR Awards from the Mutual Fund Education Alliance (MFEA), an industry organization that recognizes excellence in marketing campaigns. She aspired for us to join that distinguished group of award winners. I bought in, as long as our primary focus was driving more investments for our mutual funds, not gunning for awards. Over the next four years, we won more than fifteen STAR Awards. I highlight a few of them below, including the problem we were trying to solve, how we solved it, and the final result. A couple of these examples seem pretty basic now, but when we were launching them from 2008–2011, they were cutting edge for business-to-business marketing.

DYNAMICALLY-TAILORED EMAIL CONTENT

Context: Our mutual fund family was comprised of more than thirty mutual funds, but not all the funds were available for investment by each of our partner firms. We wanted to tailor the emails we sent to advisors and include only relevant information about funds they were invested in and others that were available to them. Our goal was to increase engagement of advisors with our emails and grow investments in our mutual funds.

Action: We worked with email service provider ExactTarget and our agency ddm marketing & communications to develop customized content and merged that with advisor details from our customer relationship software. The advisor email pulled in performance stats about their active funds, their total investments with our fund family, and details about funds we wanted them to consider.

Result: This approach demonstrated that advisors who engaged with our marketing emails had 30 percent+ higher sales than those who didn't.

FOUR PODCASTS AND THE MUTUAL FUND FAMILY COMMUTE

Context: We were a lesser-known, mid-sized mutual fund family with a relatively new name. We needed financial advisors to not only recognize our name but also to trust our expertise enough to add our funds to their client accounts. Fortunately, our funds performed well, but we just didn't have sufficient brand recognition.

Action: At the time, I was reading and listening to resources to help me think more innovatively about marketing. The "Marketing Over Coffee" podcast featured several experts informally conversing about marketing. In one episode, they discussed how podcasts were coming back (this was early 2010), not as a way to make money, but as a way to deliver information conveniently to a target audience. They also mentioned that the average commute was twenty-three minutes, the perfect time to listen to a podcast.

A lightbulb went off. Our bigger competitors provided a ton of monthly market commentary, typically in the form of multi-page reports or white papers. I decided to create five-minute podcasts for advisors to learn our firm's perspective on each of the equity, fixed income, and international markets.

I also combined those individual podcasts into one, customized the name with each mutual fund, and called it "The Commute."

Result: Within a year, our podcasts saw a collective 4,000 downloads a month. We didn't have a download goal at first, but if listener response had been disappointing, we would've shut production down. The benefit that we weren't even thinking about was that these podcasts helped our sales team share with advisors what our portfolio managers were thinking about the markets. That might have even been more important than the monthly downloads.

LAUNCHED IPAD APP, ENABLING CONSULTATIVE SALES APPROACH

Context: In 2010, the standard way the sales team would prepare for meetings with advisors was to determine which funds might interest them most and compile printed fact sheets and commentaries to launch the conversation. With more than thirty mutual funds, the sales team couldn't predict which funds might pique the advisors' interests. This resulted in the sales team looking like it was just trying to sell a mutual fund, rather than understanding what might best serve advisors and their clients.

Action: In the fall of 2010, Jim (our Head of Distribution) realized that the iPad was going to be a game changer, but he didn't know how. He bought one for each of our marketing team members and told us to figure out how it could be useful. After familiarizing ourselves with the new device, the team decided to create our own iPad app to present detailed information about our mutual funds (fact sheet, commentaries, etc.) as well as our market commentary.

Result: After we had developed a pilot version, I was traveling with a few members of our sales team. During a meeting with a financial advisor, our sales team member pulled out a folder and started reviewing our mid-cap value fund and our investment grade bond fund. The advisor asked, "What are you guys doing with munis (municipal bond funds)?" Our team member wasn't prepared to go in-depth about that fund, but he shared some high-level information. We had a great muni bond fund, so this could've been a huge missed opportunity.

Luckily, I had the iPad app and pulled up details about our muni bond fund. He was then able to meaningfully answer the fund advisor's questions.

Within nine months, nearly half of our sales team used the app in over 75 percent of their meetings. We considered that a huge success.

This is just a sampling of how I engaged throughout my career to push through the tough health moments so I could return to work (even when my bosses thought I should take longer to recover). Without my "no place I'd rather work and nothing I would rather be doing" philosophy, I might have struggled to persevere.

Summary of Career

Just as God has been faithful through all my health issues, He has been incredibly faithful when it comes to my career. I have been so fortunate. This is also an area where I have counterbalanced the negatives of my various health issues. A challenging and rewarding career has helped me focus on engaging work rather than fixating on my health. I have seen many friends struggle with negative experiences in their careers, including situations where their role was eliminated through downsizing or the sale of their company. I have never lost my job and had to endure the stress of trying to find a new one.

I have transitioned from company to company and role to role to remain challenged and energized. When I couldn't say "There is no place I'd rather work and nothing I would rather be doing," I have identified a new role where I could say that. My bosses have generally let me exercise my strengths and provided me the freedom to make decisions and learn from my failures. When I look over my career, I couldn't ask for a better journey.

Section IV

Faith and Service

The final area of my life that is responsible for the bulk of my optimism is faith and service. Realizing that I'm not the center of the universe and that not everything is about me, my needs, and my desires has been life-changing. If I'm not the center of the universe, then what is, and how does that impact how I should live?

My Christian faith is at the core of my being and the central basis of my optimism. I believe that the Christian God is a personal God who created me in His image. I believe that I am an imperfect sinner, which risks separating me from a perfect God who cannot associate with sin. I believe that, because He loved me so much, He sent His son Jesus to die on the cross for my sins so that I can live in heaven with Him for eternity. I believe that as Jesus was dying on the cross, he was 100 percent man and 100 percent God. This means that he wasn't dying for hypothetical sins that would happen in the future. He could see all of my actual sins, and he was dying for those. For him to love me that much—that he would die for me—what would I not do for him?

When Jesus was asked for the greatest commandment, he said, "You shall love the Lord your God with all your heart and with all your soul and with all your mind. This is the great and first commandment. And a second one like it. You shall love your neighbor as yourself" (Matthew 22:37-39). That leads to service, loving my neighbor as myself, and paying special attention to those neighbors who have needs I can help meet.

In the final chapter, I'll talk about the strengthening of my faith over time as well as how service has impacted my life.

Chapter 10

I Am Not the Center of the Universe

Everyone has faith in something. The question is: what is your faith in? The beginning of my faith journey is likely similar to many kids who grew up in Christian homes in the 1970s and 1980s. I grew up in the church and learned that sin had separated me from God, but He sent His son Jesus to Earth to live a perfect life and then die an excruciating death in order to pay the price for my sins. Because of what Jesus did, I have an opportunity to be reconciled with God and eventually live in heaven with Him after I die. I just need to believe in Jesus, accept him into my heart, and then, in response to what he has done for me, try to live a life that would please him. I do not try to "earn" my way into heaven. Jesus already did all the work. I simply try to live a life pleasing to him because of my gratitude for what he has done for me. When I was eight years old, I prayed a prayer to accept Jesus into my life.

I had the tremendous benefit of a mom who guided me spiritually and a church (College Hill Presbyterian Church in Cincinnati) with tremendous youth programs and leaders. Even with all of this, in my junior high and high school years, I vacillated between following Jesus and doing my own thing.

When I left for Vanderbilt, I ditched church and focused on having a good time. As my fraternity's social chairman, I spent my time planning parties, organizing swaps with sororities, and drinking—lots of drinking. In my sophomore year, what I thought was bronchitis was a heart virus that landed me on the heart transplant list. Being confronted with your own mortality can upend your perspective. I realized that my faith in Jesus was way more important than what I was doing, and I renewed my focus to live a life that would please Him.

That was short-lived. After transferring to the University of Cincinnati and connecting with that campus's fraternity, I reverted to my old ways. The fraternity brothers dubbed me "The Drunken Tinman" because I had needed a new heart like the Wizard of Oz character. I would take my immunosuppressant medications with a beer. Honestly, I drank a lot of beers before and after taking the meds. I wanted to fit in and belong, but I also realized I didn't want to be that guy anymore. In my junior year, I stood in front of the brothers at a chapter meeting and told them that the guy I had been for the past year was not the guy who I really was. I was a Christian guy who was going to do what Jesus wanted me to do. Although that wasn't the prevailing mindset among my fraternity brothers, all of them respected my courage for speaking up.

Post-college, I have focused on deepening my relationship with God and strengthening my conviction in what I believe. My life verse is Proverbs 19:21, which says, "Many are the plans in a person's heart, but it is the Lord's purpose that prevails." I am a Type A person who makes plans and executes them, so this can be a hard verse for me, but I know that God has a perfect plan for my life that is far better than I can even imagine. Every time things don't go as I planned, I remember this verse and know that He has a purpose for it that I just may not yet understand.

I've deepened my relationship with God and strengthened my convictions in three primary ways: individual study, study and fellowship with a small group, and consistent participation at church (corporate worship). Each of them is critically important, but my commitment to each has varied over time.

INDIVIDUAL STUDY AND WORSHIP

Christians believe in a personal God who wants to have a relationship with us and wants us to spend time with Him. We often refer to this time as a "quiet time" in which we can spend time reading the Bible, reading or listening to devotionals, praying, etc.

You would think that, given that I believe God sent His Son to die for my sins, I would have no problem setting aside part of my day—maybe thirty minutes—to deepen my relationship with Him as He wants me to do. Not so much. This is the area of my faith where I am weakest: demonstrating the discipline to take 1/48th of my day to build my relationship with Him. Taking medical leave from work has helped because I don't feel rushed all the time to move to the next task, but even now I sometimes find myself plowing through my quiet time so I can watch my murder shows like "The First 48" and "Cold Case

Files." That shows you how screwy my priorities can be sometimes.

Another way I spend time with God is by listening to worship music. So many songs speak to God's love for us, His sacrifices for us, and His grace and mercy towards us. I am frequently overcome by emotion when I listen and am reminded of what He has done for me. A current favorite of mine is "Scandal of Grace," performed by MBL Worship and written by Hillsong. A few of the lyrics include:

Grace, what have you done?
Murdered for me on the cross
Accused in absence of wrong
My sin washed away in Your Blood
Too much to make sense of it all
I know that Your love breaks my fall
The scandal of grace
You died in my place
So my soul will live . . .

STUDY AND FELLOWSHIP WITH A SMALL GROUP

I've learned over time that I struggle to "go it alone" when it comes to my faith. I rely on a group of like-minded people not only to be there for each other in the good and bad times, but also to challenge each other and hold each other accountable to live a life that would be pleasing to God.

Currently, three groups help me do this: a men's discipleship group, a couples' Bible study and fellowship, and a couples fellowship. Each group plays an important but slightly different role in my life.

My current men's group includes a pastor from my church, a doctor, two retired businessmen, a small business owner, and me. We range in age from our 50s to 80s, and each of us brings a different set of life experiences and perspectives to our group. What we have in common is that we all love Jesus and are doing our best to live a Christian life. We meet on Friday mornings to catch up on each others' lives, to read scripture, to discuss a book we might be reading together, and to pray. A men's group is important for me because we spend time discussing what it means to be a Godly man, a loving husband, and a good father.

The couple's Bible study that Sandy and I belong to is a little more homogeneous than my men's group. We are almost all in our mid-50s to early 60s and have kids in various stages of moving from young adults to adults. Sandy and I are the "young married couple" in this group, as we have only been married for twenty-two years. One huge benefit for us as the youngest couple is that we benefit from the wisdom of others who might be just a half step ahead of us. The group meets weekly to discuss various Christian topics, catch up on life, and pray for each other, whatever the current challenges and blessings may be.

We've known many of these couples for years, but we have been meeting as a group for six or seven years. We met the leaders of the group (Anthony & Pamela) when we moved to Atlanta in 2006. Our son was eighteen months old, and Sandy was six months pregnant with our daughter. Sandy and I had visited the Sunday School class at a local church that Anthony and Pamela were leading. When I mentioned to Anthony that Sandy was pregnant and had been early with Owen, Anthony asked, "Who has your back?" I didn't have an answer. We didn't know anyone close who could help. The good news is that Anthony and Pamela have had our back for our entire time in Atlanta.

The third group is a couples' group focused on fellowship. All six couples attend the same church, but the connection point is really our kids. We are all at the same stage of life (late high school/early college-aged kids), and most of our kids either go to school or play sports together—or both. We meet about once a month for dinner and conversation.

Although each group is different, they all rallied around Sandy and me through the transplant process. Prayer was a given across the groups, as were meals, assisting with our daughter, and housekeeping help. We found it much easier to maintain optimism with this loyal army supporting us through the stress.

CORPORATE WORSHIP

"And let us consider how we may spur one another on toward love and good deeds, not giving up meeting together, as some are in the habit of doing, but encouraging one another—and all the more as you see the Day approaching." Hebrews 10:24-25

Corporate worship—going to church—is an important part of being a Christian since it provides an opportunity to connect, encourage, be challenged, learn, and worship with other believers. During COVID and over the six months after my second transplant, I had a hard time just watching services online. I missed worshipping with others in person, which gives me a small glimpse into what I'll experience in heaven: God's people worshiping Him together.

When you are a Christian, it's hard not to be optimistic every day, realizing that our short time on Earth, where we might experience pain and suffering, pales in comparison to the eternity that we get to spend in heaven.

"He (God) will wipe every tear from their eyes. There will be no more death or mourning or crying or pain, for the old order of things has passed away." Revelations 21:4

LIVING OUT MY FAITH THROUGH SERVING OTHERS

One way I live out my faith is by helping those in need. I benefited from great role models in my parents. Mom was constantly stepping up to help others, and Dad was extremely generous with the family's financial resources. My early days of serving were an ad hoc mix of jumping into situations to help and occasionally writing checks, especially when I was under thirty. Over time, the mix has flipped, and now I write more checks than contribute physically. Sandy and I have also become more intentional about how we use our resources to support organizations and people. Serving helps us focus on those who are less fortunate financially instead of always being tempted to "compare up" or look at those who have more than we do.

WRITING CHECKS

From when I graduated college through the first couple of years of marriage, I (and we) just didn't make much money. In my 20s and early 30s, I worked as a financial advisor, a middle school math teacher, and a nonprofit program manager. When I completed my MBA, I took a job with a decent salary, but with Sandy staying home with our son, we didn't operate with much of a margin. We tithed to the church (10 percent of my salary) and would occasionally give to a handful of organizations, realizing that our giving might prevent us from going out to dinner later.

When I took a new job in Atlanta, I received a hefty pay bump. We decided to be increasingly intentional about earmarking money to give away to whatever cause we felt led to support. I opened a bank account that I call our "VC (venture capital) Fund for Giving." We started by putting an extra 5 percent of my salary and 10 percent of any cash bonuses into this account. Over time, we have supported all kinds of initiatives, whether it be a nonprofit, a family member or friend in need, or a situation that spoke to us. As my compensation has grown over time, so has our ability to impact others.

What Sandy and I have also learned is how to be more strategic with our giving of money and time. Our preference is to give to organizations where we can also volunteer and to have strategic areas where we feel led to give. For us, our primary focus areas are organizations that introduce Jesus to young people (like Young Life and Compassion International) and those focused on people living in poverty or experiencing homelessness (like Atlanta Mission and Children's Restoration Network). Even though we are intentional about saving money to later give, our funds are not unlimited, so it helps to have criteria to evaluate new giving opportunities.

ROLLING UP MY SLEEVES

Sandy and the kids have done a much better job of in-person service in the last few years than I have. Through the Young Men's Service League (YMSL) and the National Charity League (NCL), Sandy and each of the kids have been able to volunteer with a wide range of great organizations that are helping others.

Personally, I did more of the hands-on work when I was younger, joining mission trips to areas within New York City, Chicago, Atlanta, Washington, DC, and other cities. In Cincinnati, Sandy and I volunteered with the Interfaith Hospitality Network (IHN) to help families experiencing temporary homelessness. IHN provided families with shelter, meals, workforce training, and job placement assistance. Sandy and I would go to where the families were staying (typically a church) and play with the kids to give the parents a little break. We would pack school lunches for the kids. That was the first time I realized that some of the students I was teaching might have been experiencing homelessness. Kids in the shelter were the age of my students and looked no different than the kids I was teaching.

More recently, I have focused on helping at the Atlanta Mission and Children's Restoration Network. The Atlanta Mission's vision is to end homelessness, a bold and inspiring mission. Three primary ways I have volunteered with the Mission is through offering strategic support for the President's Council, distributing race packets for its annual fundraising race, and engaging in conversation with men during lunch at The Shepherd's Inn. The latter work was the most uncomfortable, but also the most rewarding. I would drive over during my lunch hour and randomly ask a man if I could join him. Then I would ask him about his story. Sometimes, the man I joined would enjoy telling his story. Other times, we would just sit in silence for a while. I stopped participating during COVID since I was on the heart transplant list, but I still remember some of those heartbreaking stories and was glad to support those who were seeking help from the Mission.

When I realize that I am not the center of the universe and can focus on those who have different needs than me, I feel optimistic. I reflect on my blessings rather than focusing on what I lack.

Conclusion

"I have told you these things, so that in me you may have peace. In this world you will have trouble. But take heart! I have overcome the world." John 16:33

Life delivers challenges to all of us. The key is how we deal with them. My health issues have no doubt generated the most negative experiences for me. In fact, I'm trying to write this conclusion today because I have another eye surgery tomorrow for surgeons to remove the skin cancer around my eye and then grab a skin graft from somewhere to repair it. I'm not exactly sure how long my eye will be out of commission.

As I've matured and endured various negative health experiences, I've grown better at minimizing their negative impact by flipping the script and finding neutral or positive meaning in the moment. If that doesn't work, I counterbalance by focusing on positive areas of my life, like my relationships, my career, and my faith and service.

My faith is the biggest factor in helping me maintain hope through the hardest times. Knowing that my health issues will not go on forever and that I will be able to spend eternity in heaven with no more sickness, sorrow, or death is a great comfort to me. If you aren't a person who believes in God, I would encourage you to choose something long-term to fix your eyes on. Find your big picture. Being able to pick your head up and look forward to what's ahead can make all the difference.

Thank you to all who chose to read this. The writing process was sometimes cathartic. I hope that some of what you read will help you as your own story unfolds and you navigate your own challenges.

Epilogue

As I wrote the conclusion to this book, I was pre-paring for yet another surgery, this time to remove skin cancer around my eye and repair it with a skin graft. I mention it almost casually, as if it were just another bump in the road, but life has a way of chal-lenging our expectations.

As an unexpected complication to the surgery, I've lost much of my vision, and recovery is proving to be a long road. The doctors aren't certain if my vision will fully return. Suddenly, this has become the sec-ond hardest trial of my life, even more difficult than the second heart transplant or triple bypass.

Imagine writing a book about maintaining hope through life's adversities, only to face a new chal-lenge that prevents you from reading the very words you wrote. The irony isn't lost on me.

Vision loss completely reshapes your life. I can no longer drive (something I took for granted) and must rely on Sandy or others to take me places. Simple pleasures like chilling in front of the TV and going to baseball games have lost their luster as everything is a big blur.

This new reality has forced our family to recalibrate yet again. We've had to figure out new ways to navigate daily life, to find alternative sources of joy, and to maintain our sense of humor when things feel impossibly hard. I wonder some days if we'll ever feel truly settled, if life will ever give us a sustained period without significant health challenges.

As I've written throughout this book, these moments are precisely when the lessons I've developed over decades matter most. Do I get discouraged? Absolutely. At times, the cumulative weight of health challenges feels overwhelming.

Then I remember what I've learned through these thirty-five years of transplants, surgeries, and recoveries: I am not the center of the universe. I continue to remind myself that even vision loss is temporary when it comes to an eternal perspective.

If you're navigating your own unexpected challenge as you read these words, my heart goes out to you. I wish I could tell you that the hard times eventually stop coming, that there's peace waiting just over the horizon, but life doesn't work that way. The challenges never truly end.

What I can tell you is this: you are stronger than you think. The resilience you develop through today's trial will serve you during tomorrow's setback. Even in your darkest moments, you can find hope, you can experience joy, and you can create meaning.

Don't give up. Remember to take heart.

DC

Thanks

I rarely read the acknowledgements in a book myself, so I'll keep this short. I would like to thank:

Jesus Christ, who is the source of my optimism and allows me to have an eternal perspective that is compelling.

Sandy, Owen, and Julia, who are by my side each and every day.

My parents and siblings, who often dropped everything to make sure I had what I needed.

All the prayer warriors who have been in constant prayer as I have battled all of my health challenges over the past thirty-five years (Heart Sisters, CHPC folks, Moms in Prayer, small groups, and many, many more).

All of you life-long and season-of-life friends who have made my life fun to live . . . despite all the challenges (whether I was able to mention you specifically in this book or not).

The Ripples Media crew, who helped get my ramblings and reflections into a book that I think might actually be worth reading.

David Craig has spent the past 35 years facing significant health challenges, including two heart transplants, an emergency triple bypass, skin cancer tumor surgeries, and more. In that same time, he has developed the discipline to remain optimistic, achieve lofty career goals, and develop meaningful relationships through significant life challenges. In this book, David shares his framework for doing this.

David lives in northern Atlanta with his wife Sandy and their two children.